Sifat Ara Siddique

Expanding Informal Sector Activities in Dhaka City

A Case Study of Education Coaching

Anchor Academic
Publishing

Siddique, Sifat Ara: Expanding Informal Sector Activities in Dhaka City. A Case Study of Education Coaching, Hamburg, Anchor Academic Publishing 2018

Buch-ISBN: 978-3-96067-213-5
PDF-eBook-ISBN: 978-3-96067-713-0
Druck/Herstellung: Anchor Academic Publishing, Hamburg, 2018

Bibliografische Information der Deutschen Nationalbibliothek:
Die Deutsche Nationalbibliothek verzeichnet diese Publikation in der Deutschen Nationalbibliografie; detaillierte bibliografische Daten sind im Internet über http://dnb.d-nb.de abrufbar.

Bibliographical Information of the German National Library:
The German National Library lists this publication in the German National Bibliography. Detailed bibliographic data can be found at: http://dnb.d-nb.de

© Anchor Academic Publishing, Imprint der Diplomica Verlag GmbH
Hermannstal 119k, 22119 Hamburg
http://www.diplomica-verlag.de, Hamburg 2018
Printed in Germany

**Dedicated
To
My Parents**

Acknowledgement

I want to express my deepest gratitude to various people who have made this work possible. First of all I want to thank my supervisor **Professor Dr. Nurul Islam Nazem** for guiding me through the work of this thesis, his positive encouragement and his most valuable advice. Furthermore, I would like to thank all the respondents – schools' authorities, students and their guardians, authorities of the coaching centers and the national level experts for their kind co-operation.

I think if any of us honestly reflects on who we are and how we got here; we discover a debt to others that spans written history. The work of some unknown person makes our lives easier every day. I believe it is appropriate to acknowledge all of these unknown persons; but it is even more necessary to acknowledge those people we know have directly shaped our lives.

I want to thank my family for their inspiration throughout the research and beyond. Family includes for me not only my relatives. My life wouldn't be what it is without my friends. Thank you for enriching my life with your fellowship.

October, 2017

Sifat Ara Siddique
Author

CONTENTS	PAGE NO.

LIST OF FIGURES

ACRONYMS

H.S.C	Higher Secondary Certificate
S.S.C	Secondary School Certificate
ILO	International Labor Organization
EBSEB	East Bengal Secondary Education Board
SBA	School Based Assessment
MBA	Master of Business Administration
UGC	University Grant Commission
MoE	Ministry of Education

Abstract:

The study of urban informal sector education has gained importance and expanded the scope and contents of the study in last thirty years. One of the major challenges of geographers to find the dynamics of this sector, as it is expanding gradually and a huge number of students are related to this activities. This research examines the role of education coaching as an urban informal activity. Dhaka city as a center of education has been experiencing the proliferation of coaching centers since last twenty years. The mushrooming of coaching centers is symptomatic of the failure of our education system as a whole. Formal education institutions are failing to provide the students with necessary instructions at the classroom. This is why the guardians and their wards are making a beeline for education coaching. This research aims to describe the process of growth of coaching centers as an informal sector activity with a special emphasis on students' involvement in this process. As an empirical research, it follows detailed questionnaire survey and direct interview method. This study discusses the size of economy controlling by the coaching centers, students' dependency on coaching and the impact of this phenomena. It has been found in the study the study that parents' concern and desire for better result play important role to students' involvement in coaching. About 96.67 percent students take extra education coaching. It concludes that this informal sector activity is creating a negative impact on our education system and there is much room for further research to explore different aspects of this activity.

Keywords: Informal sector, education coaching, formal education, students, dependency on coaching.

CHAPTER ONE

GENERAL INTRODUCTION

1.1 Introduction

Informal sector is that part of an economy which is beyond official recognition and record and which produces productive, useful and necessary goods and services without formal system of control. Informal sector activities constitute a major part of the urban economy in the Third World countries like Bangladesh. It provides employment more than 60 percent of the labour force (Islam, 2010). Bangladesh is an overpopulated country. Population growth rate of Bangladesh is about 1.54 percent and growth rate of population of the capital city Dhaka is about 4.2 percent (Population Census, 2001). This unusual growth of population in Dhaka have been due to various factors such as natural increase, migration from rural to urban and migration from other cities owing to greater attraction of employment. But the formal sector is not sufficient to provide services to the increasing population. So, people have to engage themselves in the informal activities. As a result, different types of informal activities are flourishing day by day in the city. Education Coaching is one of them. It has been operating in the city both in informal and semi formal manner. The pattern and process of its growth and development is directly or indirectly linked with the space, history, culture and socio-economic condition of the country. This study will focus on the growth and development of the sector as well as the nature and students' dependency on this informal activity.

1.2 Statement of the problem

Education coaching is one of the fundamental problems for the development of our national education system. It is however, not a new phenomenon. It has been practicing for ages through in different forms and under different circumstances. It is very interesting and at the same time a subject of deep concern that in recent decades there have been substantial increases of coaching centers in Dhaka city. At present it has sprung out all over the city as an informal activity. Students cannot think of getting an admission at any level- from primary to the highest seat of learning without going through this coaching centre, which is a threat to our education system. The impact of this informal activity is quite visible in our society and reflected as a negative consequence for the education system as well as urban economy.

Education is the gradual process of acquiring knowledge. It is widely recognized that education serves as an engine for the community. It plays a vital role in all around development of the society. Earlier economists argued that the purpose is to produce competent human resources in order to develop a state (Kotler, 2006). In 1980's scholars argued that the purpose of education is to train its consumers in order to contribute both in economic and social human needs contexts which will ultimately provide a balanced national development. Modern and contemporary education is necessary for this development. It has increased the quality of education. But at the same time it has created an opportunity for marketization of education in the form of coaching, which is unethical.

The informal sector has been growing in Dhaka city in such a way that it can no longer be considered as a temporary phenomenon. Coaching centre has become one of the largest informal activities of the city where investment is nominal but the return is phenomenal. An incongruous and irrelevant situation is found in the city of Dhaka and it is expanding fast in other cities and towns of the country which seems to be very unethical. We cannot deny this situation as time has created this situation. The existence of so many coaching centers sketch the practical situation of the education system of our country. Probably the government does not have or very little control over these institutions. They remain isolated from the existing government rules. However, there has been little investigation and research on urban informal sector education in Bangladesh, and those studies are not adequate to explain the problem and prospect of this sector. So, it needs a scientific study to explain its dynamics in terms of economy, employment generation and students' dependency on this sector.

1.3 Definition of the informal sector

The informal sector is an important addition into the economy of Third World country. The informal sector as its name suggests is not formal in character. Thus the economic activities in any field not formally recognized by the authority may be included activities under informal sector. In the absence of a clear definition, the concept remained hazy and boundaries were indistinct. The picture began to clear in 1971, when Keith Hart compiled a list of income earning opportunities among resident of a slum area in Accra in Ghana, in which he contrasted the informal income earning opportunities with that of formal sector. The distinguishing characteristic used was wage earning employment as against self-employment. Sethuraman(1976) provides a useful direction by suggesting some multiple criteria for identifying informal enterprises. These are: (1) the enterprises distribute output directly to the consumer, (2) members of the household head of the enterprise work in it, (3) it does not observe fixed hours of operation. However, in search of workable definition of the informal sector, the concept developed by the International Labour Organization (ILO). During early 1970s, the ILO enunciated the concept of the informal sector which was regarded as having the following characteristics:

- Non wage earning
- Unauthorized and unregulated operation
- Labour intensive and adapted technology
- Non formal sources of education and skills
- Reliance on indigenous resources

Informal sector consists of small scale units engaged in the production or distribution of goods and service operated whether on individual or household basis with the primary objectives of generating employment and income to the participants notwithstanding the constraints on capital.

Over the last 35 years, the ILO in particular has presided over, conducted and sponsored hundreds of studies to better understand the myriad of social, economic, environmental and political issues relating to the informal economy in the cities. Most of this research has been focused on cities in less developed countries. There is a wide variety of informal activities ranging from micro to macro level. Most of these activities have evolved from local necessity and unemployment situation. These activities have both advantages and disadvantages.

In 2002, the ILO defined the informal economy as "all economic activities by workers and economic unit that are – in law or in practice – not covered or insufficiently covered by formal arrangements" (ILO 2002). The new definition broadens the focus from just looking at the characteristics of unregulated enterprises to include unregulated wage earners and employment relationship.

1.3.1 Towards the Definition

Education coaching as an informal activity has been practicing in the country for ages. But the practice was very limited in the past. Then it was not viewed as a part of economy. But in recent decades, the proliferation of these coaching centers has compelled the researchers to consider it as a part of informal economy. However, education coaching has a different form. Generally, they are operating in three forms- in organized coaching centers, coaching in teachers' home and private tutors in students' home. Two types of education coaching are found in the city- academic coaching and admission coaching. Coaching for different classes and different subjects and for exam preparation coaching is included in academic coaching.

Admission coaching provides special coaching for school, college, and university and MBA admission. However, they have no authority to provide formal certificate. Some of the coaching centers have trade license and pay tax to the government, but the vast sector is operating in an unregulated manner. Official recognition and security of employment is absent. At the empirical level, education coaching as an informal activity is defined to comprise those enterprises which satisfy one or more of the following conditions.

- Easy entry in the job market
- Lack of formal educational qualification
- Low wages and does not have any fixed wage structure
- Does not observe fixed hours of operation
- Does not have fixed number of employee
- No official recognition and job security
- Unregulated and competitive market

1.4 Aims and objectives

The aim of this study is to understand the process of growth of coaching centers as informal activity and its role in the economy. It aims to identify the condition under which they absorb students and generate employment and income. It also aims to investigate if there would be any relationship between formal sector institutions and informal coaching centers. More specifically, the objectives of this research are:

1. To study the size of economy the coaching centers control in the city.
2. To estimate what proportion of students come through these coaching centers.
3. To study the process of getting students' involvement as well as the pattern of development of coaching centers in the informal sector activities.

1.5 Significance of the Study

Geographers ask what factors control the pattern of distribution of a phenomenon and the impact that the phenomenon creates on the space. The more advanced an urban economy is, the greater the inevitability of the shift of economic activity from informal to formal spheres. Based on this assumption, Third World cities like Dhaka will generate more informal economic activities than the more advanced urban counterparts in more developed countries, and are therefore more worthy of research. Thus the significance of the study lies in the fact that enormous coaching centers have been established on the base of Dhaka and their service is becoming valuable for the students. Millions of students are getting informal services from them. Many people including the teachers and the students are involved in this process. The money, generated from the sector is also phenomenal. However, little is known about the dynamics of this sector in terms of its process of development and pattern of activities. It is necessary to understand this sector whether the sector stands as counter pole of the formal education sector. This study is an attempt to find out the total process of the sector as an informal activity in the city.

1.6 Conceptual framework of the study

An informal economic activity is one which is unregulated, unregistered, and does not pay tax to the government. Cumbersome entry procedures push entrepreneurs into the informal economy, where businesses pay no taxes and many of the benefits that regulation is supposed to provide are missing. As a result different types of informal activities are found in the city. Education coaching is one of them. It is operating both in formal and semi formal way. That is why it is very important to know the determinants of the activity. The study considers the size of this informal economy, growth of coaching centre and students' involvement to these coaching centers. The following diagram is considered for the development of education coaching in the informal sector:

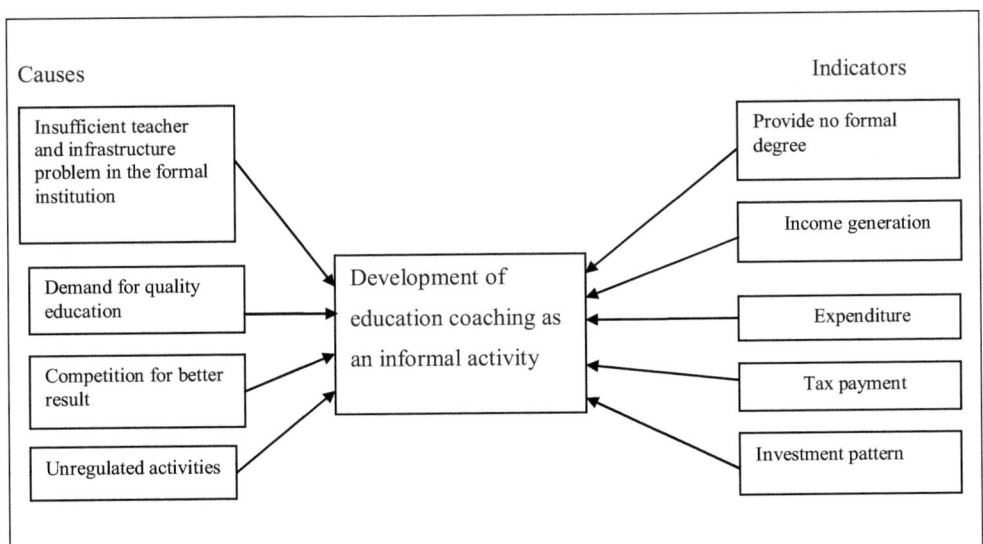

Figure 1: Cause and indicators that create a condition for the development of education coaching as an informal activity.

1.6.1 Explanations of the key variables

• Problems in the formal educational institution: Problems in the formal educational institution create a situation for taking extra education coaching. Two major problems of many government and non-government are insufficient teacher and inadequate infrastructure.

• Demand for quality education: Education is necessary for all kind of development. And demand for education is increasing with the increasing number of population. But sometimes formal educational institutions cannot fulfill this demand. So, students have to take extra coaching. As a result, coaching centers are growing.

• Competition for better result: Competition has been increased for better result to get access to better educational institutions. For this higher class, middle and higher middle class families send their wards to the coaching centers.

• Unregulated activities: A leap frog development of education coaching has been found in recent decades. Government has no control over them. They are doing their activities in an unregulated manner.

• Income generation: Income generated by an informal activity is a good indicator to measure its size of the economy.

• Expenditure pattern: Education coaching is a different type of informal activity. Its expenditure pattern for its consumer will provide information about the range of services.

• Tax payment: Informal enterprises are characterized as informal because they rarely comply with tax payment. So, it is an indicator to identify the nature of education coaching as an informal activity.

• Investment pattern: Most of the informal activities invest very low amount of money for starting its business. Investment pattern reflects the process of growth of these activities.

1.6.2   Process of Getting Students' Involvement

Like many others informal activities, it is very difficult to sketch the pattern of its development and the process of its operating system. Different types of coaching have evolved to serve different purpose. But the process of getting students' involvement is more or less same. Following diagram will depict the process of getting students' involvement

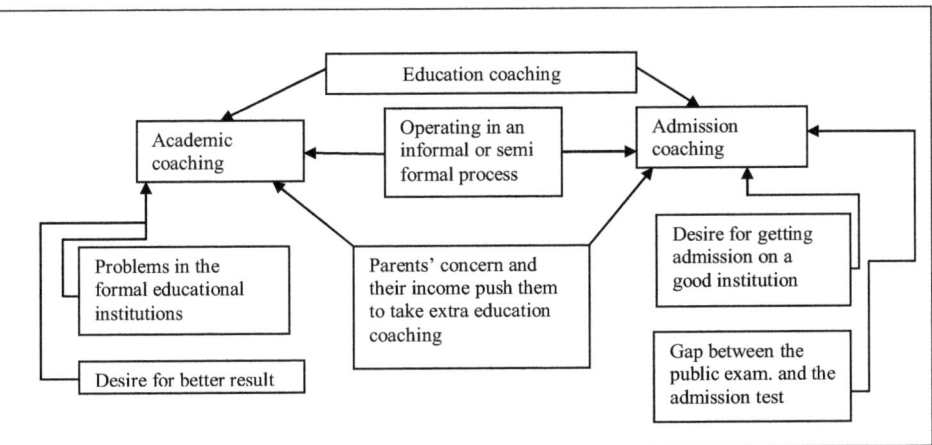

Figure 2: Students' involvement (as service receiver) in this sector

The role of education is to develop human resources, build the nation and making linkage between knowledge and empowerment. Education should be a means to empower people to become active participant in the community. Education must be the right of the citizens not their opportunity. But what actually we see the privileged ones in the society have the right and opportunity whereas the neglected section receives very scantly of education.

Dhaka city, the nerve centre of business, commerce and education of the country, hosts people of various categories. But the number of education institutions is not adequate to serve the demand of these people. The wards of middle and higher middle class study in privately established educational institutions. But to get wards admission into these institutions seems to be nightmare ordeal to the guardians. After getting admission into these institutions, guardians have to bear a constant headache till the wards pass the public examination due to various unhealthy practices developed in these institutions over the year

Due to the limited seats in these institutions many deserving candidates are deprived of admission facilities which throw the guardians into a world of despair. After the admission every students bound to read three or more private tutors which claims three or four times more expenditure than that of usual tuition fee.

For getting admission a little kid is also to undergo a hard admission test and the contents of one test are quite unmatchable for their age. These standards are getting tougher and tougher. And guardians are getting more conscious and competitive minded. As a result coaching is evolving in our education arena.

1.7 Research Hypotheses

Informal activity is the largest sector of urban economy by employments. There is a growing appreciation among scholars in urban development and design, especially those involved in the 'Everyday Urbanism' movement (kaliski,1999), of the informalization of urban space driven largely by informal economic activities. Informal activities and its variation have compelled academics to define their impact on urban environment. Education coaching is one of them. It is providing service to the education sector in an informal way. This research tries to identify the spatial pattern of this activity and the processes that are involved in the development of this pattern. The research has the following hypotheses:

H_1: Problems in the formal educational institutions are positively associated with the growth of extra coaching activities.

H_2: Students' family income is directly related to their involvement in the extra education coaching.

H_3: Students' results are positively related to their engagement in the education coaching.

1.8 Methodology of the Study

Different types of coaching centers are expanding in the city but no information is found about their process of development and operating system. The research has been conducted under the topic of "Expanding Informal Sector Activities in Dhaka City: A Case Study of Education Coaching". All empirical research in such field must be exploratory not only because of the problems of definition but also because of the lack of adequate statistical information. The research methodology followed in this study is therefore exploratory. Both qualitative and quantitative approach has been applied for the nature of investigation and circumstances of the research topic.

The study has been conducted according to the following sequences:

1. Relevant literature from secondary sources was reviewed to outline the nature of the problem of informal sector with particular reference to education coaching.
2. Number of education coaching in Dhaka City was collected from the secondary sources.
3. Twenty coaching centers have been selected for the detailed study.
4. Finally, a questionnaire survey was undertaken to generate primary data for the study.
5. Relevant expert opinion has been taken.

1.8.1 Source of Data

The secondary sources include published materials and official documents like books, journals, magazines, newspapers, reports, leaflets etc.

Primary data were collected in several stages, by conducting questionnaire surveys. The first target was to select coaching centers of different categories to collect information about their growth and development process. Thus, the first stage of primary survey was to choose coaching centers at various locations.

The second target was to collect information from students about the reasons for taking extra education coaching. The students from higher classes at secondary level were selected.

The third stage of questionnaire survey was a follow-up study with the guardians after getting information from the students.

The fourth stage of primary investigation was in-depth interviews that are conducted with the experts and intellectuals. The experts were chosen from various disciplines as well as occupational categories.

1.8.2 The Study Area

The study focuses on the present situation of education coaching as an expanding informal activity in Dhaka city. Thus, the whole Dhaka city is the study area. However, the study needs to generate primary data from appropriate respondents. So, it is necessary to select educational institutions as well as coaching of various types from different location. In terms of location, it would have been ideal; if those were selected from all over the city. Due to limitation of time and resource, the researcher considered three educational institutions and twenty coaching centers.

Among the educational institutions a boys' school, a girls' school and a combined (both boys' and girls') category school are selected. The institutions are- Government Laboratory High School, Agrani Girls' School and New Poltan Line School and College. These three institutions are chosen for various reasons. The reasons are: One of them is government and others are non-government schools. Government Laboratory High School and Agrani girls' School are renowned in the city but New Poltan Line School and College is unfamiliar. In order to get diversified information they are selected.

Twenty coaching centers are selected from different location of the city. It is very difficult to depict the actual statistics of an informal activity like education coaching. However, scanning of their advertisement, promotional activities and others unpublished documents, the researcher identified that around one hundred and twenty three coaching centers are operating in the city. Among them ten academic and ten admission coaching are selected. This sample will help the researcher to understand and extract different information related with the process of development and size of economy controlled by the coaching centers.

1.8.3 Selection of the Respondents and Sample Size

1. Students and their guardians: 240 cases are selected through 480 (240 students and 240 guardians) questionnaires as this sample size can easily be manageable. Among these half are for boys and half are for girls. Half of the students are from class VIII and half of them are from class X. The students have been selected from higher class (class VIII and class X) so that they can give information properly. Another reason for selecting students from this level is that they can understand their needs and they have their own views for taking extra education coaching. The guardians are interviewed in order to get insight into the subject matter.

2. Coaching Centers: 20 cases are selected for detailed study. Ten admission coaching of different categories and ten academic coaching of different categories are selected. Thus the variation will help to provide diversified information about the development education coaching as an informal activity.

3. National level experts: The respondents at the national level were selected from a cross section of people attached to the field of education and research. Twenty experts are selected. The researcher tries to consider all the stakeholders related to this field.

Map 1: Location of Selected Schools

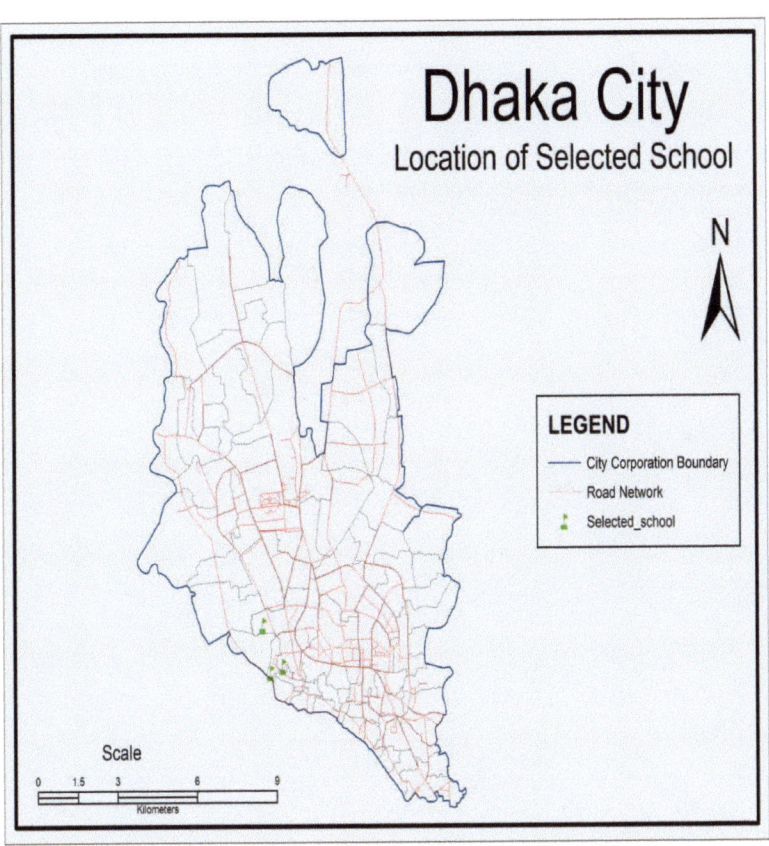

1.8.4 Questionnaire Design

Questionnaire is designed in four categories to extract data from four levels of respondents.

First, the questionnaire is designed for the students considering the variables that cover information related to the process of getting their involvement to the coaching centre. It also seeks to find out the relationship between their results and engagement in the coaching centre. The questionnaire is semi-structured in nature.

Secondly, the questionnaire is designed for the guardians. It covers information related to the occupation, monthly income-expenditure and reasons for sending their wards to the coaching centre. It seeks to find out that if there would be any relationship between students' family income and their involvement to the extra education coaching. The questionnaire is open-ended in nature.

Thirdly, the questionnaire is designed for the authorities of the coaching centre. It covers the information related to the investment pattern, income generated by the coaching centre, expenditure pattern for the students etc. It tries to investigate the size of economy controlled by the coaching centre. It is semi structured in nature.

Finally, the questionnaire is designed for the national level experts. It seeks valuable opinions of the experts on the total processes of the sector as an informal activity.

1.9 Research Design

Following diagram shows the research design as well as methodological approach followed in this study

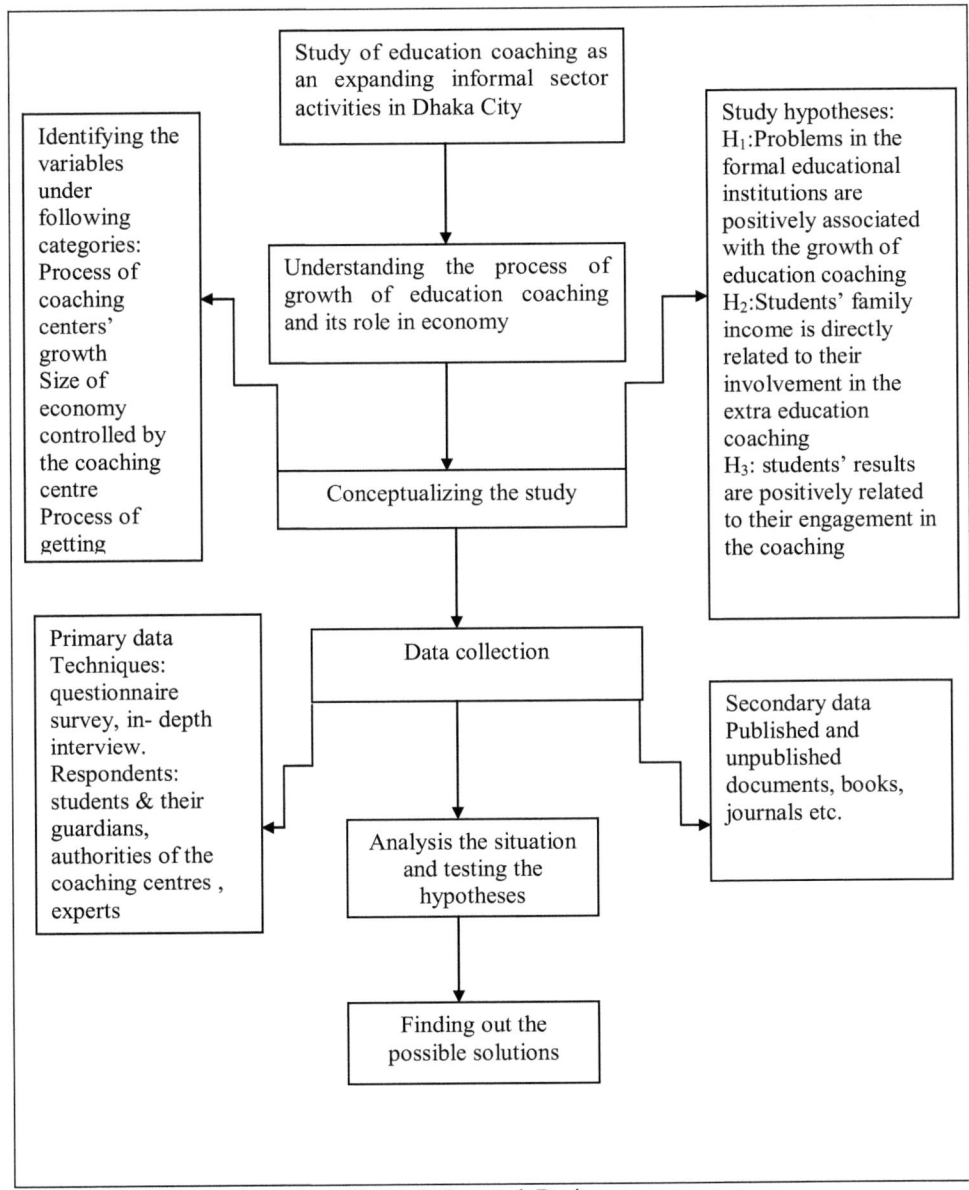

Figure 3: Research Design

1.10 Scope and Limitation of the Study

Geographers seek to establish generalizations by observing and analyzing diverse phenomena to detect uniformities underlying their diversities. The establishment of generalization makes possible to predict the probable consequences of specified occurrence. The task of geographers is complicated by the multiplicity of the focus acting simultaneously on the phenomena they investigate. The depth and significance of the geographical generalization depends on the quality of the underlying observation and analysis.

It is very difficult to sketch the informal activities in a single frame. Education coaching is not different from it. Different types of education coaching have different characteristics. But some common causes create the situation for the development of education coaching. It will be ideal if all coaching centre were selected. But it is obviously impossible to address all the education coaching. Their actual statistics is not available. So, the researcher has to rely on their advertisement, promotional activities and others unpublished documents. Generally it is found that most of the coaching centers do not want to give their financial information. Authorities always try to avoid their responsibilities.

The present study mainly focuses on the growth and development of education coaching in the informal sector activities as well students' involvement to this process. This study will help the geographer to analyze unban informal economy in a different way.

1.11 Organization of the Thesis

This thesis organized in seven chapters. The first chapter has introduced the research problem, objectives, conceptual framework, significance and methodology of the present research. Second chapter discusses the evolution of coaching centers in our education system. The third chapter provides insight into the growth and development of education coaching and students' involvement to this sector. Determinants of the size of the economy have been discussed in fourth chapter. Fifth chapter highlights different factors that are involved in the process of growth of education coaching and tests the research hypothesis. Sixth chapter reflects the opinion of selected national experts on the impact of education coaching. Finally, chapter seven summarizes the whole study.

CHAPTER TWO

EDUCATTION SYSTEM IN BANGLDESH AND EVOLUTION OF COACHING IN THIS SYSTEM

2.1 History of Education in Bangladesh Perspective

The concept of learning throughout life is the key that gives access to the 21st century. It goes beyond the traditional distinction between initial and continuing education. It links up with another concept, that of the learning society in which everything affords an opportunity for learning and fulfilling one's potential (Aggarwal, 2000). Bangladesh has a long history of organized education dating back to eras when many of the modern, developed countries were still passing through the ignorance of dark ages. The focus of this chapter is to the history of education in our country and evolution of coaching in this system. This history can be divided into different periods. Education was introduced in the sub-continent by different processes in these periods.

Ancient period: In the early Vedic period (2000-1000 B.C.) education was a family responsibility. Father or older member of the family taught other members of the family. In the later Vedic age (1000-500 B.C.) education was institutionalized by a process known as Gurukul. In this period Brahmic education entered Bengal. At that time Guru-Shissho (teacher- pupil) system was very popular. An individual with a good analytical knowledge was considered as Guru (teacher) and his followers are known as Shissho. Exercising knowledge through Guru-Shissho had always been a fundamental part of education in Bangladesh. Gurukuls were traditional Hindu residential school of learning. Guru's home was the school where pupils lived for the whole period of education as a member of the family. Education was free but students of well-to-do families paid 'Gurudakhshina', a voluntary contribution after the completion of their studies. At that time, education was confined to the elite group.

Gurukul usually received the state support in the form of allotment of rent free land. But Guru had full autonomy to decide what to teach and how to teach. The curricula showed that Gurukul provided both general and occupation oriented courses (Banglapedia, Vol 5, pp.444-458).

Raymont's definition of education was appropriate for that time. According to Raymont, education means the process of development in which consists the passage of the human body from infancy to maturity, the process whereby he gradually adopts himself in various ways to the physical, social and spiritual environment (Raymont, 1963)

Towards the end of ancient period two types of school were developed - The tol or pathsala and network of indigenous elementary school. In the later part of the Brahmic period, Buddhist education began to expand.

Buddhist period: In this period, education took on a different shape. One main difference was that it was that it was not based on Vedic study. It was open to all and there were strict regulations for the conduct of pupils towards the teacher. In this system, the pupil rendered the services required by the teacher. In turn, the teacher gives the pupil all possible intellectual and spiritual help and guidance by teaching and instruction. The most important Buddhist Bihara (centre for learning) was Nalanda which was famous for its learning. Two such residential Bihara were developed in Bangladesh- Paharpur (Naogaon) and Moinamoti (Comilla).

Muslim period: In Muslim period (1204-1600 A.D.), Bengal was ruled as a province of Mughal empire and sometime it was an independent state. The rulers established maktabs and madrashas as educational institutions. Madrasha education was free. The teacher enjoyed high status in the society. The courses of madrasah generally included religious subject. Women during Muslim rule did not have opportunity for education due to 'PURDA' system. But there are evidenced that women of noble family received education in their houses from teachers. This was perhaps the first form of coaching.

British period: British records show that indigenous was widespread in 18th century. Before the introduction of a formal school system in many British colonies and similar regions, privileged parents would employ private tutors known as lodging master to educate their children. This was home based coaching. One of the important events of this period was the endorsement of Macaulay's Minute in Lord Bentink's dispatch of 7 March 1835, which provided that western learning should be spread through the medium of English language. Use of English as medium of instruction in public education was announced as a formal policy. As a result, a good network of English high schools and colleges were established in Bengal, mostly due to government initiative and support.

Pakistan period: After British rules, the demand for education was increased and formal schools became popular. The first task of the government of East Bengal within the framework of independent Pakistan was to readjust vacuum created in the educational scene of the province due to large scale exodus of Hindu teachers, administrators and staff to India. To fill up the gap, the government of East Bengal promulgated the East Bengal Educational

Ordinance 1947 following which the former Dhaka Board of Intermediate and Secondary Education was replaced by a new East Bengal Secondary Education Board (EBSEB) and immediately, all high schools came under the control of this board. In those days, there were not too many schools in the villages. Boys interested in education had to move out from their own village and take lodging in village nearer to a school. In the cities, the system was somewhat different. People did not like keeping lodging masters for a variety of region. They used to hire tutors who would visit their houses for a fixed period of time and teach for a salary. At that time, private tuition was not so common. Only a few students who found themselves weak in one or two subjects used to take private tuitions from their school or college teachers.

Bangladesh period: After the independence, there has been an increase in formal education provision though most acknowledge that education should be the fundamental concern of public policy (Alam, 2008). Educational administration and management is run by the Ministry of Education in association with four departments and directorates as well as a number of autonomous bodies. For the secondary level of education, there are seven Boards of Secondary and Higher Secondary education and a Madrasha Education Board. The University Grant Commission was created in 1973 to coordinate the activities of the universities and allocate government grant. The government of Bangladesh took initiative to formulate education policy and formed Education Commission. From1972 to 2003, five education commissions were formed. Three education policies were constructed. With the gradual increase for the demand for education in Bangladesh, the numbers of educational institutions as well as the number of students were also increased. At that time, education coaching both informal and semi formal form began to flourish. Teachers found it as an extra source of their income. Before 2001, The Bangladesh Education System was generally marks-based. Students, seeking good marks took private tuition in teachers' houses. Sometimes they kept tutors in their home. After the introduction of grading system, the competition for good result had increased. From then, rapid expansion of coaching centers opened the geographic segmentation of marketing in order to provide the service of target group. Besides the teachers, other people took that opportunities and opened coaching centers with eye catching signboards. Now it has turned out as a business.

2.2 Dhaka: A Center of Education

Dhaka's emergence as an educational centre owed much to the geographical location and owed much to the cultural heritage of its hinterland. In the 19th century, Dhaka had not only become the main centre of education, but also the second largest centre of education in the province ranking only after Calcutta (Ahmed, 1986). During the Mughal period, Persian and Arabic education were introduced in Dhaka. At that time, there were a large number of Hindu who were high officials, priests, teachers and landholders. Besides, knowing Sanskrit they also learnt different types of languages for serving administrative purpose. With the establishment of British rule, English education was necessary to enter into the new world of intellectual discovery and challenges. Western education scarcely got under way before 1835. Till then education remained traditional in content and method. The first people to meet the new educational needs of Dhaka were the Baptist Missionaries of Serampore. In 1815, they sent R. Owen Leonard to Dhaka to establish an English school. In 1816, the first English School near Chauk Bazar was established. He also founded seven Bengali schools. This was the beginning of formal school in the city. At that time, many people kept tutors in their house for learning English language. Dhaka's growth as educational centre was further aided by the new educational system of the 1850s. There had been considerable changes of direction in the progress of education. Numerous educational institutions were established during that time. Establishment of those institutions caused great excitement in the city and tension between conservatives and progressives. From that time, there evolved a competition for quality education. City people did not like lodging system. Few people took private tuition to fulfill their needs. Coaching in a commercial was totally absent. Center based education coaching has evolved in recent decades. And large scale proliferation these coaching centers make them as an informal sector activity of the city.

2.3 Background of Coaching Centers' development

According to Oxford Advanced Learner's Dictionary (2010), the word coaching means to train or teach the students for the preparation of examination. The word coaching has entered into our education system from the beginning of Pakistan period. At that time, schools provided especial coaching for the preparation of S.S.C examination. But at present, the concept has been changed. Outside of the school, professional teacher or non professional people have opened coaching centre to fulfill the extra need of the students in a commercial way. This is the present form of coaching centre.

The socio-economic and political condition of the country is responsible for the evolution of coaching centres. The most harmful and self destroying approach is the insufficient investment in the education sector. Because of the fragile infrastructure, many students are deprived from the proper education. Many meritorious students do not come to this profession due to lower pay scale. Moreover corruption has increased in the education sector. As a result many teachers were recruited in an unfair way which deteriorated the quality of education. Due to lack of facilities in the school, students take the help of extra education coaching.

Private tuition was seen in British and Pakistan period. But that was very few in number and considered as a disgraceful activity. But after independence, the situation has been changed. Population of Bangladesh has been increased in manifold and demand for education was also increased. As a result many incompetent people had joined in this profession. Informal private tuition took the shape of business oriented coaching centre as a semi informal form. The commercial approach in education coaching was started in first half of 1980s. First commercial coaching centers were established for Cadet College admission. Very soon varsity admission coaching was started. It was incepted by some student organizations. Their objective was not commercial, rather they wanted to collect student for their organizations.

From the middle of 1980s, admission coaching became popular among the students. This has inspired some people to open academic coaching for different classes. Since then coaching centre has been proliferating all over the country.

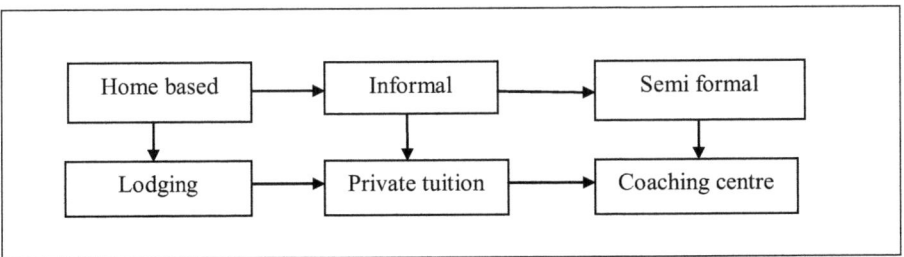

Figure 4: Changing the pattern of education coaching from home based to semi formal form.

2.4 Impact of Education Coaching on Society

Education coaching has polluted the noble purpose of the education. At present many of the students and guardians think that the purpose of education is to pass the examination or to secure good marks only. Coaching centre provides guidebooks, suggestion paper, hand note the students and teaches short-cut techniques of securing good marks. Thus, it reduces the creativity of the students. This situation depicts an ominous picture of our education system. Millions of investment in education sector becomes ineffectual for this reason. Because, just raising the rate of literacy does not indicate massive development in the education sector. This is a threat to our society.

2.5 Commercial Aspect

Many students fulfill their extra need from the coaching centre. Coaching center is also increasing day by day as the competition has been increased in education arena. The owner of coaching center invest very little amount of money but they earn phenomenal amount. On the other hand guardians spend lion share of their income for these coaching. Most of the coaching centres are informal and semi-formal categories. They do not provide any formal certificate. Most of the coaching centres do not pay tax to the government. At present, it is one of the largest informal activities in the city which sometime act as a counter pole to the formal education system. The National Education policy, 2010 discourages the practice of private coaching. Government is trying to put a bar on private coaching (The Dally Star, 22nd August, 2010). But the task is gigantic and challenging.

CHAPTER THREE

EDUCATION COACHING AS AN INFORMAL ACTIVITY: ITS DEVELOPMENT AND STUDENTS' INVOLVEMENT IN THIS ACTIVITY

3.1 Introduction

Informal sector plays a controversial role in urban economy. It creates employment opportunity but offers poor job security and in many cases jobs are low paid. Informal activities are well known for their heterogeneous characteristics. Describing the characteristics of informality for the purpose of generalization is not easy because the border between the formal and informal sector is hazy. Most of the economic activities start with informal characteristics then they take the shape of formal activity. Education coaching as an informal sector is a significant but not well understood phenomenon. It has been practicing years after years in our country. It was emerged from a home based shape and now operating in different shape. At present, it is one of the largest informal activities of the city that fulfils the extra educational need of the large number of people. This chapter is designed to explore the characteristics, development process of this activity as well as students' involvement in this activity.

3.2 Education Coaching in Dhaka City

Dhaka City is the commercial and educational hub of the country. Renowned schools, colleges and universities are situated in the city. Large numbers of students come from different parts of the country for getting admission on those institutions. But the formal institutions are limited in proportion with the number of students. As a result competition has been increased. Taking this as a benefit numerous coaching centers have been developed in the city. These coaching centers are found both in commercial and residential area. But it is difficult to find out the actual number of these coaching centers. The vast sector is operating in an unregulated manner. It is almost impossible to identify the number of private tutors and group coaching; as they do not use any identity. Only organized coaching centers are identified through their commercial promotional activities. Present study found only one hundred and twenty three coaching centers that have a registration number or membership of Bangladesh coaching centers' association. The actual number may be more than that which cannot be identified due to limited scope.

Map 2: Distribution of Coaching Center in Dhaka City

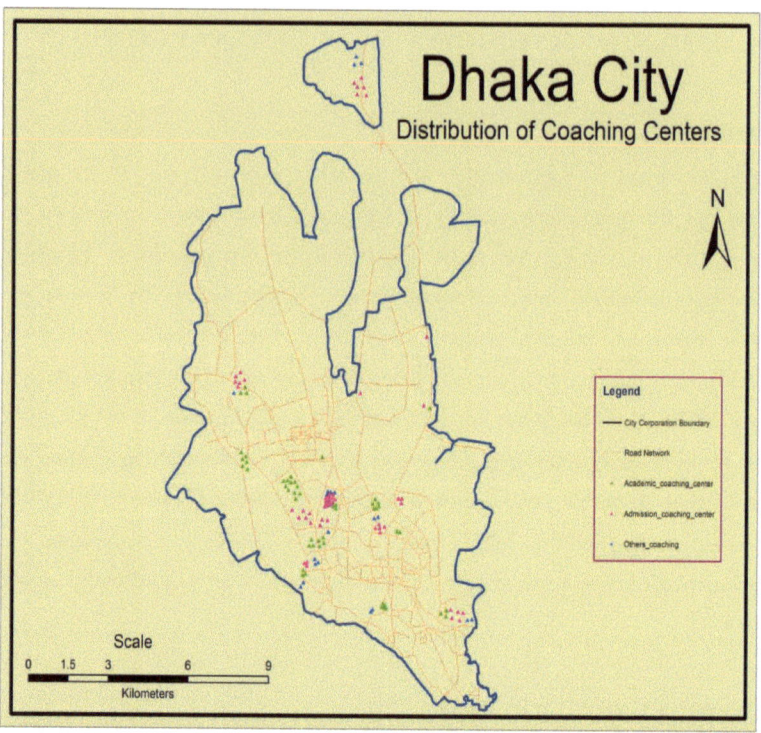

3.3 General Characteristics

Education coaching emerges from the poor socio-economic condition of our country. In the past, poor school teachers take it as an extra source of income to cope with their necessity. Time has changed the form and shape of this activity. At present it is one of the profitable businesses rather than a survival activity. However, it covers a wide range of activities that include different nature. For example, it is considered as a survival activity for the teacher (low paid) and educated unemployed people in an economic environment where earning opportunities are limited. But at the same time large entrepreneurs try to escape labor regulations and other institutional regulations.

The workforce of education coaching can be categorized into following groups

1. **Private tutor**: generally, he teaches students in their house. Private tutor can be considered as own account worker who own and operate one person business.

2. **Group/ batch coaching's teacher**: he teaches students in a group or batch in his house. Sometimes, family members help him.

3. **Organized coaching centre**: it is an institutionalize shape of coaching. More than one teacher serves here. These coaching centers have owners who employ paid teachers according to their needs. Most of the time, they desire to escape labor regulations.

However, twenty organized coaching centers have been selected for detailed study to understand their characteristics and nature of growth.

3.4 Types of Coaching Centers and Their Branches

Heterogeneity is a common matter that exists among different types of education coaching. In a personalize format, a single person may be the coach, teacher or guide. But when organized coaching centers are considered, variation in different segment of the coaching is found. Organized coaching centers are of two types- Academic coaching and Admission coaching.

Academic coaching is of two types- class wise coaching and subject wise coaching. Class wise academic coaching offers courses for different classes. Most of these coaching centers offer courses for class IV to class XII. Some of them start their services from nursery class. Subject-wise coaching offers courses for different subjects. English, Mathematics, science based subjects (physics, chemistry, biology etc.), commerce based subjects (accounting, statistics etc.), and Bangla are usually taught here.

Admission coaching is another form of education coaching which is popular among the students. It has different forms. It ranges from school admission coaching to higher level education. Currently school admission coaching has closed their services as government has changed the admission system for class I students. College admission coaching operates for a very short period of time only two or three months. Usually they offer courses after S.S.C. examination and then close after publishing of S.S.C result. Rest of the months these coaching centers act as an academic coaching. Some them remain closed. Other form of coaching is graduate level admission coaching. Perhaps it was the pioneer of business oriented coaching centers though it was not started with these motives. Graduate level admission coaching is of different types. These are: university admission coaching, medical admission coaching, engineering admission coaching.

Range of service differs from one coaching centers to another. Admission coaching centre's range of service is larger than academic coaching centre. Academic coaching has fewer branches than admission coaching. Sometimes academic coaching provides service for small portion of students. But the admission coaching centers targets larger portion of the students and expands their business according to these policy. Study shows that most of the coaching centers have their branches in and outside of Dhaka city. In Dhaka city 40 percent coaching centers have branches that range from three to five. 25 percent (5 out of 20) coaching centers have more than 25 branches outside of the city. However most of the coaching centers try to catch larger target groups and expand their service all over the city. Main branch (head office) tries to control other branches in the city. Those branches depend on their main branch for any kinds of business and policy oriented issue. But main branch has less control over other branches outside of Dhaka city. Outside of Dhaka, the branches use the goodwill and share a percentage of profit with main branch. Only few of them depend on their main office for policy oriented issue.

Table 3.1: Number of Branches in Dhaka of the surveyed Coaching Centre

Number	Frequency(n=20)	Percentage
Less than 3	4	20
3-5	8	16
6-8	5	25
More than 8	3	15
Total	20	100

Source: Field survey, 2011

Table 3.2: Number of Branches outside of Dhaka of the surveyed Coaching Centre

Number	Frequency(n=20)	Percentage
No branches	7	35
Up to 10	2	10
10- 25	6	30
More than 25	5	25
Total	20	100

Source: Field survey, 2011

3.5. Location of the Coaching Center

Location is an essential factor for the survival of any kind of informal activity. Most of the time accessibility plays an important role to determine the choice of location. Study shows maximum numbers of coaching centers are situated in Farmgate area. It is one of the busiest commercial areas of the city. It is also an easy accessible place of the city. It is an area where varieties of informal activities are found. In 1980s, when first coaching centers were established, Farmgate was emerging as a fast growing commercial area. So, it is apparent that any kind of business activity will take this benefit and choose the location for their establishment. Their main concern was how to create demand and survive their business in a fast growing city. Soon they became successful to create a demand for education coaching. When it became a profitable business, many other coaching centers agglomerate in the same place, then expanded all around the city. This time expansion and choice of location was more logical than previous. Coaching centers expand their branches around different school and college. Their leapfrog development pattern is found in and outside of the city.

Map 3: Location of Selected Coaching Center

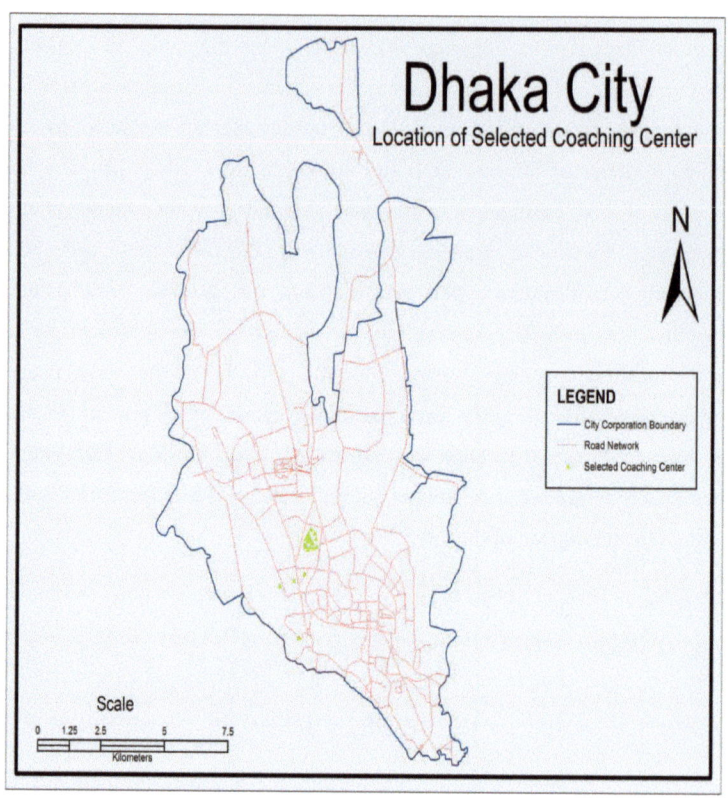

Map 4: Branches of coaching centers' outside of Dhaka

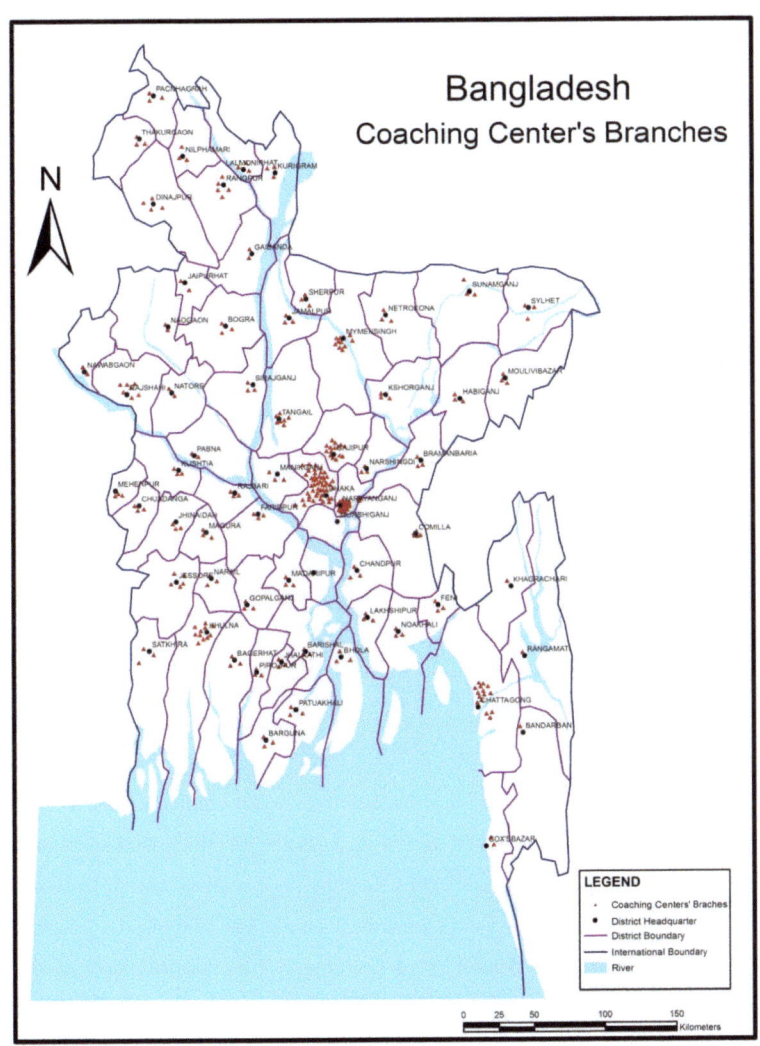

3.6 Nature of Employment

Lobour employment is one of the significant factors of informal sector activity. Coaching centers have three types of employee- permanent, semi-permanent and temporary in nature. Like other informal sector activities, most of the employments in the coaching centers are temporary. Labour regulation does not maintained here properly. As mentioned earlier, main branch has little control over other branches beyond Dhaka; only branches of the city are considered here. Study shows that most of the coaching centers do not have fixed number of employee. Total number of employee varies with their range of services. Coaching centers with few branches have little number of employees that ranges up to 50. Large coaching center can employ more than 130 employees. Survey result shows that 20 percent (4 out of 20) coaching centers have more or less fifty employees; other 20 percent have more than 130 employees.

Table 3.3: Total number of employee of the coaching surveyed centre*

Number	Frequency(n=20)	Percentage
Up to 50	4	20
51-80	5	25
81-110	2	10
110-130	5	25
131 & above	4	20
Total	20	100

*number of employee considers only the branches of Dhaka

Source: Field survey, 2011.

Total number of employee is not fixed because maximum employees are temporary. Twenty is the highest number for permanent employee whereas it is the lowest number for temporary employee. Study shows that 30 percent coaching centers have sixteen to twenty permanent employee and 20 percent have more than twenty employees (Table 3.4). 25 percent coaching centers have twenty to forty employees but another 25 percent have more than eighty employees as their range of services cover different parts of the city (Table 3.5).

Table 3.4: Number of permanent employee of the surveyed coaching centre

Number	Frequency(n=20)	Percentage
Up to 5	3	15
6-10	4	20
11-15	3	15
16-20	6	30
20 & above	4	20
Total	20	100

Source: Field survey, 2011

Table 3.5: Number of temporary employee of the surveyed coaching centre

Number	Frequency(n=20)	Percentage
Up to 20	3	15
21-40	5	25
41-60	3	15
61-80	4	20
81 & above	5	25
Total	20	100

Source: Field survey, 2011

3.6.1 Teachers of the Coaching Centers

Teachers are temporary or semi permanent employee of the coaching centers. Most of the teachers do not have any kind of formal training or professional degree to teach the students. All the coaching centers recruit graduate level students as teacher. They are the active employee of this sector. Few coaching center recruit retired school (25 percent) and retired college teacher (10 percent). Sometimes school and college teachers teach in these coaching centers. Study shows that 20 percent school teachers and 15 percent college teachers serve in the coaching centers.

Table 3.6: Teachers' qualification of the surveyed coaching centre *

Salary	Frequency(n=20)	Percentage
Retired school teacher	5	25
Retired college teacher	2	10
School teacher	4	20
College teacher	3	15
University students/ medical students	20	100

*multiple responses are considered
Source: Field survey, 2011

Teachers do not get fixed salary. They are paid lecture wise. It depends on the duration of lecture and qualification of the teachers. Generally, professional teachers get higher salary than student teachers. Study shows that it ranges from taka100 per lecture to taka500 per lecture. 60 percent (12 out of 20) coaching centers pay taka300 per lecturer and 40 percent (8 out 20) coaching centers pay taka500 per lecture.

Table 3.7: Salary for the teacher surveyed coaching centre *

Salary	Frequency(n=20)	percentage
100tk per lecture	2	10
150tk per lecture	5	25
200tk per lecture	4	20
300tk per lecture	12	60
500tk per lecture	8	40

*multiple responses are considered
Source: Field survey, 2011

3.6.2 Others Staffs of the Coaching Centers

Besides the teachers coaching centers have two types of staffs – director and managerial staffs. Director is the owner of the coaching centers. .He is permanent. Sometimes coaching center has two or more directors who share the business. He takes honorarium from the coaching center. It ranges from more or less taka 40,000 to above taka 80,000. Study shows that 50 percent coaching centers gave taka 40000to taka60000 to their directors (Table 3.8). Managerial staffs are permanent or semi permanent. Their salary is not fixed. Salary depends on their working hours. They have no fixed hour of operation. Only few coaching centers gave a monthly salary to their permanent managerial staffs. Only 35 percent coaching centers gave more than 10,000taka and another 30 percent gave 80,000taka to 10,000 taka to their managerial staffs (Table 3.9).

Table 3.8: Honorarium for the Director of the surveyed coaching centre

Salary (Taka)	Frequency(n=20)	percentage
Up to 4000 0	3	15
40001-60000	10	50
60001-80000	5	25
80001& above	2	10
Total	20	100

Source: Field survey, 2011.

Table 3.9: Salary for the managerial staff of the surveyed coaching centre

Salary(Taka)	Frequency(n=20)	percentage
Up to 4000	1	5
4001-6000	4	20
6001-8000	2	10
8001-10000	6	30
More than 10000	7	35
Total	20	100

Source: Field survey, 2011.

3.7 Students' Involvement as a Service Provider in This Sector

Students are the main workforce in this sector. Generally university students and medical college students serve in the coaching center. In this globalized world everything is getting expensive. Education expenses are also increasing day by day. In such situation, student wants to be self dependent. Easy entry in this sector creates immense opportunity for them. Most of the graduate level students involved in this sector and take it as an extra source of their income.

3.8 Students' Involvement as a Service Receiver in This Sector

If education is considered as a service product, then first consumer of this product is the students. Organized coaching centers have only thirty years old history. When they started their activities 45 percent of them have only five or less than five students. Only one coaching centre (out of 20) is found that had students more than twenty in their base year (Table 3.10).

Table 3.10: Base year students number of surveyed coaching centre

Number	Frequency(n=20)	Percentage
Up to 5	9	45
6-10	4	20
11-15	4	20
16-20	2	10
More than20	1	5
Total	20	100

Source: Field survey, 2011.

But with the increasing of student's number, competition has been increased. Considering this as an opportunity, coaching centers began to expand their services an soon they became successful to attract more and more students. Their last year and current year students' number show students are being dependent on their services.

Table 3.11: Last year (2010) students' number of surveyed coaching centre

Number	Frequency(n=20)	Percentage
Up to 500	1	5
501-1000	2	10
1001- 1500	2	10
1501-2000	1	5
2001-2500	1	5
2501-3000	2	10
More than 3000	11	55
Total	20	100

Source: Field survey, 2011

Table 3.12: Number of students enrolled in coaching centers surveyed 2011

number	Frequency(n=20)	percentage
Up to 1000	2	10
1001- 1500	2	10
1501-2000	0	0
2001-2500	1	5
2501-3000	1	5
More than 3000	12	60
Total	20	100

Source: Field Survey, 2011.

3.9 Conclusions

Although, coaching centers sometimes show the characteristics of formal activity, they fulfill most of the criteria of informal activity. Their rapid expansion proves that they are successful to create their demand in the society. Students are getting informal services from them. Large portion of the students are dependent on this sector. Therefore, for a greater benefit of the nation we have to think that how to improve formal education system and reduce the dependency on education coaching.

CHAPTER FOUR

DETERMINANTS OF THE SIZE OF THE ECONOMY

4.1 Introduction

Estimating the size of economy controlling by education coaching is problematic because of its heterogenic nature. It has viewed earlier that no two coaching centers have similar characteristics. Their size of economy also varies from one another. Major determinants that are used to determine the size of economy are income, expenditure and investment pattern. The focus of this chapter is to sketch the size of economy controlled by the coaching centers in the city.

Primarily, twenty coaching centers have been chosen for detailed study. They were asked about their income, expenditure and investment pattern. But most of them felt uncomfortable with these questions and tried to escape actual answer. Then 240 students from two different classes were interviewed to know their expenditure on education. However, from two separate checklists an attempt has been taken to depict size of economy of these coaching centers.

4.2 Income Generated by the Coaching Centers

Only source of income of this coaching center is the fees that they collect from the students. It has been found from the study about 232 students (out of 240) take extra education coaching. Most of the students take more than one coaching and they have to spend more money for it. Table 4.1 shows students' expenditure for extra coaching.

Table 4.1: Distribution of expenditure (per month) on education coaching

Expenditure(in Taka)	Frequency(n=232)	Percentage
Up to 1000	13	5.6
1001-2000	51	21.98
2001-3000	36	15.52
3001-4000	35	15.09
4001-5000	32	13.79
5001-6000	28	12.07
6001-7000	26	11.2
7001& above	11	4.74
Total	232	100

Mean = 3642
Source: Field Survey, 2011.

41

The expenditure starts below taka1000 and ranges above taka7000. On an average students have to spend taka 3642 per month for extra education coaching. Table reflects coaching centers' income pattern from two different classes (class VIII and class X). But the range differs for other classes. It indicates that large amount of money is rolling in this sector. Different coaching centers collect fees in different ways. But three common ways are- admission fees, course fees and subject fees. Besides this, sometime they arrange especial program and charge extra fees from the students.

Admission fees: Depending on the types and quality of services, accommodation facility, duration of services, admission fees differ from one coaching centers to another. Academic coaching runs almost all the year round but admission coaching operates for a few months of the year. They start their activities after H.S.C and remain closed after finishing of graduate level admission in different universities and colleges. They charge higher fees than the academic coaching. Full course fee is taken as the admission fee. It ranges from 6000taka to above 8000taka. Study shows that 40 percent coaching centers charge above 8000taka. All of them are admission coaching. Academic coaching takes fewer fees. But they take monthly course fee and subject wise fee.

Table 4.2: Admission fee of the surveyed coaching centre

Academic coaching		
Fee (Taka)	Frequency	Percentage
Up to 500	2	20
501-1000	2	20
1001- 1500	2	20
1501-2000	2	20
2001-2500	2	20
Total	10	100
Admission coaching		
Fee (Taka)	Frequency	Percentage
6001-7000	2	20
7001 -8000	4	40
8001 & above	4	40
Total	10	100

Source: Field Survey, 2011.

Course fee: Courses offered by the coaching centers vary for different classes. Monthly course fees are not fixed. It depends on the duration of the course. Academic coaching offers their courses from class IV to class XII. Higher classes have to pay higher course than other

Table 4.3: Course fee (monthly) of the academic coaching centre (multiple responses)

Class	Fee (Taka)	Frequency (n=10)	Percentage
IV-V	Up to 2500	5	50
VI-VII	2501-3000	8	80
VIII	3001-3500	7	70
IX-X	3501-4000	4	40
XI-XII	4001 & above	4	40

Source: Field survey, 2011.

Subject wise fee: Some of the coaching centers collect subject wise fees from the student. Study found that students take coaching for fourteen subjects. Among them, English (70.69 percent) and mathematics (86.64 percent) are most demandable subjects (Appendix 2, Table: 1). Subject wise fees vary from one coaching center to another. Generally, it ranges below 300 taka to above 500taka (Table: 4.4). Within a coaching it can vary for different classes and for different subjects.

Table 4.4: Subject wise fee of the academic coaching centre surveyed (multiple responses)

Fee(Taka per subject)	Frequency (n=10)	percentage
Up to 300	5	50
301-400	8	80
401-500	5	50
501& above	4	40

Source: Field Survey, 2011.

4.3 Investment Pattern

Like other informal activities, coaching centers do not invest very much. They have to invest very little amount of money for starting their business. They need an office space to run their activities. Most of them rent the space. So, it is very easy to start and expand the business. Study found that only coaching center (out of 20) has their own office building. Rent of their office building starts from below taka 40000. Table 4.5 shows that 55 percent coaching centers share this range. An extreme case is found. Only one coaching centre has to pay above taka 100,000 for their office building as it occupies the whole apartment.

Table 4.5: Rent of office building (head office) of the coaching centre surveyed

Rent(in taka)	Frequency(n=20)	Percentage
Up to 40,000	11	55
40,001- 60,000	5	25
60,001-80,000	1	5
80,001-100,000	1	5
100,001 & above	1	5
Not applicable*	1	5
Total	20	100

*Not applicable indicate that it own the building

Source: Field Survey, 2011.

4.4 Expenditure Pattern for the Students

Providing a good service is the principle ethics of any kind of business. Coaching centers are not beyond of this ethics. To capture the target group they use promotional activities and provide other services. They use leaflets, banner, signboards, and advertisement to catch the target group. Study shows that all the coaching center use leaflet. They distribute these leaflets in front of different school and colleges. 65 percent (13 out 20) coaching centers use banner and signboard.

Table: 4.6 Nature of the promotional activity*

Promotional activity	Frequency(n=20)	Percentage
Leaflets	20	100
Banner & signboard	13	65
Wall painting	8	40
Advertisement on newspaper	7	35

*multiple responses are considered

Source: Field Survey, 2011.

Most of the coaching centers (17 out of 20) think that through the promotional activity they can catch their target groups. So, they spend large amount of money for this purpose. Table 4.7 shows per year cost of promotional activity.

Table 4.7: Cost of promotional activity (per year)

Cost(in taka)	Frequency(n=20)	Percentage
Up to 50000	2	10
50001- 100000	5	25
100001-150000	6	30
150001-200000	4	20
200001 & above	3	15
Total	20	100

Source: Field Survey, 2011

Study shows that 30 percent coaching centers spend more than 100000 taka for promotional activity and 15 percent coaching centers spend more than 200000 taka for the same purpose. This is the only sector where they spend large amount of money for their students.

Coaching centers provide some other services. But they do not keep accounts the cost for those activities or perhaps they do not want to disclose their register. Table 4.8 shows other services that are frequently offered by the coaching centers.

Table 4.8: Services provided by the coaching centre *

Services	Frequency(n=20)	Percentage
Lecture-sheet/ hand notes	17	85
Guide books	7	35
Suggestion	20	100
Hostel facility for the students those are outside of Dhaka	3	15

*multiple responses are considered

It is apparent from the table that all the coaching centers provide suggestions and 85 percent of them provide lecture-sheet or hand notes. Students said these service charges are included in their fees. Three admission coaching centers offer hostel facility as large portion of the students come from different parts of the country during graduate level admission period.

4.5 Net Turnover per Year

To achieve maximum profit is the main condition for the survival of any kind of business. Coaching is a profitable business. Without spending much amount of money, they earn a phenomenal amount. Study shows that seven coaching centers have 11 to 15 percent turnover per year and five coaching centers have more than 20 percent turnover per year. On an average net turnover of these coaching centers is 14 percent.

Table 4.9: Net turnover per year of the surveyed coaching centre

Net turnover (Percent)	Frequency(n=20)	Percentage
Up to 5	1	5
6-10	5	25
11-15	7	35
16-20	2	10
21 & above	5	25
Total	20	100

Mean _ 14 percent
Source: Field Survey, 2011

4.6 Conclusions

Most of the informal activities try to survive as they have low profit. But the size of economy of these coaching centers shows that huge amount of money is rolling in this sector. It is one of the largest informal activities in the city. Proper steps should be taken so that the coaching centers cannot avoid existing rules and regulation of the country.

CHAPTER FIVE

STUDENTS' DEPENDENCY ON EDUCATION COCHING

5.1 Introduction

It has been indicated in the preceding chapters that how education coaching is expanding day by day. The main cause of expansion is that it has created a demand in the society. In this chapter, an attempt is made to look into the factors, which relate to students' dependency on education coaching. It has been found that competition among the students and demand for quality education is high in the society. But educational institutions are limited in proportion with the increasing number of students. Moreover, teacher-students' ratio is high in most of the educational institutions. It is therefore, important to know why students are being dependent on coaching, and what factors are influencing them to take extra education coaching.

First, students from three schools were asked about the reasons for their dependency on education coaching. It was assumed that since the students were of aged 14 and above they were able to answer the question of their extra educational needs. Secondly, students' parents and guardians' were interviewed about their decision for sending their wards to the coaching centers. In addition, respondents' economic condition were also studied.

A number factor has been found which play an important role in the dependency on coaching center. In most cases a number of factors worked together. The factors were grouped into following categories.

5.2 Social Factors

Education is the foundation of excellent human resource in a country. Education can provide solution for any kind of social, political and economic problem. So, demand for education is increasing day by day. This has been reflected in the present study while investigating the social factors. The factors are as follows

5.2.1 Educational Background of the Parents

It has been observed that higher educated parents do not think that there is a necessity of coaching in our education system but most of them send their wards to the coaching centers. Perhaps they are bound to follow the system of education coaching. Only 3.33 percent (8 out of 240) parents do not send their wards to the coaching.

Table 5.1: Level of education of the parents and guardians of the respondent students.

Education level	Father		Mother		Not sending their children to the coaching	Sending their children to the coaching
	N=240	Percentage	N=240	Percentage		
Primary	2	0.83	15	6.25	--	
Secondary	8	3.33	31	12.92	--	
S.S.C	28	11.67	44	18.33	--	
H.S.C	45	18.75	58	24.17	--	232 (96.67)
Bachelor	38	15.83	68	28.33	--	
Masters	110	45.84	24	10	8 (3.33)	
Others	9	3.75	0	0	--	
Total	240	100	240	100	240 (100)	

Source: Field Survey, 2011.

Table 5.1 shows the relationship between educational backgrounds of the parents and children's enrolment in the coaching. It can be observed from the table that mothers' educational qualification is an important factor. Higher educated mother do not prefer to send their children to the coaching though the percentage is very little. Different reasons act as controlling factors for sending their children to the coaching centers. Most of the parents (45 percent) think that better result can be achieved by sending their children in the coaching (Table: 5.2). 17.5 percent (42 out of 240) parents confess that they do not have enough time to help their students in their study. Parents also complain that school can not complete the syllabus (9.58 percent) and it is not providing enough education (8.75 percent) to their children. Some parents send their children for better understanding of lesson (9.17 percent) and other send to fulfill extra educational need (9.58 percent). It has also been found that 6.25 percent parents think that their children will be more attentive if they attend education coaching.

Table 5.2: Distribution reasons behind sending their wards to the coaching *

Reasons	Frequency (n=240)	Percentage
For better result	103	45
Sometime students cannot understand classroom lesson	23	9.58
Parents don't have enough time to help their wards	42	17.5
To fulfill extra need	23	9.58
For better understanding	22	9.17
School is not providing enough education	21	8.75
To make wards more attentive	15	6.25
School cannot complete the syllabus	23	9.58
Not sending in the coaching	8	3.33

*multiple responses are considered.
Source: Field Survey, 2011.

5.2.2 Who Influences the Children to Take Extra Coaching?

Usually it is the parents who desire to send their children to the coaching. But sometimes students themselves feel that they need extra coaching. Present study shows that students are also influenced by their teachers and friends.

Table 5.3: Source that influence the students in making decision of taking extra coaching

Source	Frequency(n=240)	Percentage
Own decision	43	17.92
Parents	115	47.92
Friends	32	13.33
Teacher	24	10
Advertisement	10	4.17
Others	8	3.33
Not applicable	8	3.33
Total	240	100

Source: Field Survey, 2011.

Though coaching centers spend large amount of money for promotional activities, it has little impact on student. Table 5.3 shows that only 4.17 percent (10 out of 240) students are influenced by the advertisement of the coaching centers. In some cases students are also influenced by the members of their family, senior students, relatives and friends' guardians. Present study identified a number reason for taking extra coaching. One common reason is to secure good marks in the examination. Another reason is that school cannot complete the curriculum; in that case they need the help of coaching. Students also complain that they are forced by their teacher or parents to take extra coaching. Some students take coaching to their relevant school teachers to get marks in school based assessment (S.B.A)

Table 5.4: Reasons for taking extra education coaching (multiple responses)

Reason	Frequency(n=232)	Percentage
School cannot complete the curriculum	66	28.45
To fulfill extra need	55	23.71
To secure good marks	118	50.86
Forced by teacher or guardians	15	6.46
For proper guideline	5	2.16
For S.B.A. marks	4	1.72

Source: Field Survey, 2011.

5.2.3 Occupation Pattern of Guardian and Their Opinion towards the Necessity of Education Coaching

It has been found that the service holders groups think there is no necessity of coaching in our education system. Businessmen have both types of responses but most of them said coaching is necessary. Other groups also think that coaching is necessary in our education system. Table 5.4 shows that 47.58 percent parents think that education coaching is necessary in our education system. 34.08 percent (34 out of 113) parents think that education coaching is necessary for better result in the examination while another 26.55 percent (30 out of 113) parents attach more importance to its necessity as school cannot provide quality education (Table 5.5). Because of rapid finishing of syllabus in the school, sometime students cannot understand the lesson properly. In that case, parents desire to send their children to the coaching. 9.73 percent parents consider that school education is not enough for better result while 11.5 percent parents consider that coaching fulfils extra need of the students.

50

Table 5.5: Occupation pattern of the parents and guardians of the students surveyed

Occupation pattern	Frequency (n=240)	Percentage	Necessity of coaching in education system			
			Positive response	Total	Negative response	Total
Government service holder	47	19.58	--		47	
Teacher	22	9.17	--		22	
Doctor	9	3.75	--		9	
Engineer	15	6.25	--	113 (47.58)	15	127 (52.92)
Private service holder	13	5.42	--		13	
Banker	8	3.33	--		8	
Lawyer	5	2.08	--		5	
Business	80	33.33	72		8	
Shopkeeper	21	8.75	21		--	
Day labor	20	8.33	20		--	
Total	240	100	240 (100)			

Source: Field Survey, 2011.

However, Table 5.4 shows that 52.92 percent parents think education coaching is not necessary. 75.59 percent of them believe there is no necessity of coaching if school can provide quality education and 26.77 percent parents think if they can help their wards in their study, they do not need to send them to the coaching. Some guardians think that students lose their creativity because of coaching and others think that coaching means wasting of time (Table: 5.6).

Table 5.6: Guardians' response as to the necessity of education coaching

Reasons	Frequency (n=113)	Percentage
Because of rapid finishing of syllabus in the school	10	8.85
School cannot provide quality education	30	26.55
For better result	34	30.08
For better education	15	13.27
Coaching fulfills the extra need of the students	13	11.5
School education is not enough for better result	11	9.73
Total	113	100

*multiple responses are considered
Source: Field Survey, 2011

51

Table 5.7: Reasons behind negative comments *

Reasons	Frequency (n=127)	Percentage
No need if school can provide quality education	96	75.59
No need if guardians can help their wards in their study	34	26.77
Wasting of time	4	13.15
Students lose their creativity	30	23.62

*multiple responses are considered.
Source: Field Survey, 2011.

5.3 Economic Factors

Education is becoming expensive day by day. Coaching has increased the expenses in manifold. Table 5.7 shows monthly family expenditure on education and a single student's

expenditure on coaching. Family education expenditure ranges below 2000 taka to above 13000 taka. As mentioned earlier eight students do not take extra coaching, other 232 students have to spend large amount of money for coaching. It ranges up to 8000taka. It has been observed from the study that family education expenditure increase because of students' involvement in the coaching. Table shows that 14.58 percent (35 out of 240) families spend up to 8000taka for their children education, while 21.98 percent (51 out of 232) students need 2000taka for coaching.

Table 5.8: Monthly education expenditure of the parents and guardians of the student

Expenditure Level	Monthly family expenditure on education		Expenditure on coaching for respondent student	
	Frequency (n=240)	Percentage	Frequency (n= 232)	Percentage
Up to 1000	0	0	13	9.91
1001- 2000	10	4.17	51	21.98
2001-3000	23	9.58	40	17.24
3001-4000	13	5.42	35	15.09
4001-5000	17	7.08	32	13.79
5001-6000	17	7.08	28	12.07
6001-7000	22	9.17	16	6.89
7001-8000	35	14.58	11	4.74
8001-9000	20	8.33	6	2.58
9001-10000	32	13.33	--	--
10001-11000	13	5.42	--	--
11001-12000	16	6.67	--	--
12001-13000	9	3.75	--	--
13001 & above	13	5.42	--	--
Total	240	100	232	100

Source: Field Survey, 2011.

5.4 Other Circumstances

There are some other circumstances that influence the students to take extra educational coaching. These are as follows:

Institutional problem: There are some problems in our formal educational institutions. One major problem is that teacher student's ratio is very high. Present study found this ratio in three surveyed schools – 1:75; 1:65 and 1:60. It is almost impossible for a teacher to provide quality education among sixty or above students within forty minutes class. There are also some infrastructural problems. For example- the schools have libraries but the students do not have opportunity to use it. Students do not get their desire service from the formal institution. 45 percent (108 out of 240) students think that school education is not sufficient and they need extra coaching. These situations create an opportunity for the growth of coaching.

Table 5.9: Students' opinion towards formal school education

Opinion	Frequency	Percentage
Sufficient	132	55
Insufficient	108	45
Total	240	100

Source: Field Survey, 2011.

132 students think that school education is sufficient but only eight of them do not take extra coaching. Students have identified a number of reasons behind their opinion all of those indicate to the existing problems of our educational institutions (Table: 5.9 & Table: 5.10).

Table 5.10: If sufficient, then why take coaching (multiple responses)

Reasons	Frequency (n=132)	Percentage
To secure good marks	43	32.58
To increase knowledge	19	14.39
To fulfill extra need	31	23.48
For better understanding of lesson	20	15.15
School cannot complete the syllabus	14	10,6
Too short class hour to solve problem	6	4.55
All teachers are not cordial	15	11.36
Forced by parents	3	2.27
Sufficient but not effective	6	4.55
For better competition	4	3.03
Not taking coaching	8	6.06

Source: Field Survey, 2011.

32.58 percent (43 out of 132) students think that formal education is sufficient but they do not get good marks through it. Another problem is that schools have too many vacations in their academic year; as a result they cannot complete the syllabus. Students also think that knowledge can be increased through extra coaching. Some of the students (6 out of 132) think that though formal education sufficient, it is not effective.

Students were asked as to know why they think formal institution is insufficient. All of those opinions depict the problems of our formal institutions (Table 5.10).

Table 5.11: Reasons behind negative responses (multiple responses)

Reasons	Frequency (n=108)	Percentage
Rapid finishing of the syllabus on the school	6	5.55
School cannot complete the syllabus	22	20.37
Not taking proper care	15	13.88
Classroom education is not enough for better result	15	13.88
School cannot fulfill extra need of the students	6	5,55
Not taking classes properly	14	12.96
Careless attitude of teacher	20	18.52
Too many students create problem for the teacher to make lesson understandable	10	9.25
Corruption	7	6.48

Source: Field Survey, 2011.

Major problems identified by the students are – school cannot fulfill their needs, too many students in the classroom create problems for students to understand lesson, too short class hour to solve problem, all teachers are not cordial etc. These problems create a demand for quality education. When formal education does not satisfy this demand, they have to depend on informal coaching. Study shows that 60.83 percent students coaching is necessary in our education system while another 39.17 percent students think it is not necessary in our education system (Table 5.11).

Table 5.12: Students' opinion towards the necessity of coaching in our education system

Opinion	Frequency (n=240)	Percentage
Necessary	146	60.83
Not necessary	94	39.17
Total	240	100

Source: Field Survey, 2011

Students were asked for major reasons behind their opinions. These reasons also reflect the major problems of our educational institutions (Table 5.12).

Table 5.13: Reasons behind students' opinion

Reasons behind the necessity of coaching in our education system (multiple responses)			Reasons behind the negative opinion (multiple responses)		
Reasons	Frequency (n=146)	Percentage	Reasons	Frequency (n=94)	Percentage
To fulfill extra need	14	9.58	Wasting of time	21	22.34
To secure good marks	24	16.44	School education is better than coaching	17	20.21
School education is not enough for good result	30	20.54	School should be more careful	15	15.96
School cannot meet the demand of students	34	23.28	Self study is enough for good result	17	20.21
Coaching is better than classroom education	30	20.54	Don't get enough time for study in home because of coaching	12	12.77
To increase knowledge	20	13.69	No answer	14	14.89
Teachers are not caring	22	15.07			

Source: Field Survey, 2011.

Table 5.12 shows that students think formal education is better than coaching and coaching means wasting of time. Some of them suggest that schools should be more careful to their students. Some students also think that self study is enough for results.

However, 132 students (out of 240), have said that formal educational institutions are sufficient but 76 students of them said coaching is necessary. 108 students (out of 240) have said formal education is insufficient and 70 of them said coaching is necessary in our education system. This demand creates a competition for better result and better education.

Students try to fulfill their need outside of formal system. Present study finds a link between problems in the formal educational institutions and the growth of coaching centers.

This research has a hypothesis: **Problems in the formal educational institutions are directly associated with the growth of coaching centers.**

Existing problems in formal institutions act as a trigger for the growth and expansion of coaching centers. Study found that problems in the formal education institutions are directly associated with the growth of education coaching; $x^2 = 1.31$ accepted at 1 degree of freedom and .05 level of confidence (Appendix 3). The most common problems are higher teacher students' ratio, infrastructural problems, limited class hours, careless attitude of the teacher, etc. students become dishearten and feel the need of extra education coaching. And taking these as an opportunity the coaching centers expand their business.

Relationship between students' family income and their involvement in the coaching: it has been said that education expenditure is increasing day by day. It is assumed that parents who have more money spend more for their children's education coaching. Present study tries to find out relationship. Table 5.13 shows income level of the family and students involvement in the coaching.

Table 5.14: Family income level and expenditure on education coaching

Income level Taka	No. of family (X)	Expenditure on coaching Taka	No. of students involved in coaching (y)
Up to 10000	11	Up to 1000	13
10001-20000	33	1001- 2000	51
20001-30000	54	2001-3000	40
30001-40000	43	3001-4000	35
40001-50000	33	4001-5000	32
50001-60000	23	5001-6000	28
60001-70000	12	6001-7000	16
70001-80000	21	7001-8000	11
80001 &above	10	8001 & above	6
Total	240	Total	232

The hypothesis is **Students' family income is directly related to their involvement in the coaching**

However, present study found that students' family income is not directly related to their involvement in the extra education coaching. It is students' need and whatever the income level, parents have to fulfill this need. This hypothesis is rejected; F= 5.138 rejected at 1 and 8 degree of freedom and .05 level of significance. Though higher income families send their children more to the coaching centers. But students who take education coaching do not consider the family income. According to their need they depend on it.

Relationship between students' result and their involvement in the coaching: One of the common reasons of all the students was that they take coaching to secure good marks. Extra coaching has an impact on their result. They are also satisfied with the service of coaching centre. Table 5.13 shows that only 18.75 percent (45 out of 240) are unsatisfied with the services.

Table 5.15: Students' satisfaction in the services of coaching centre

Opinion	Frequency(n=240)	Percentage
Satisfied	174	72.5
Moderately satisfied	13	5.42
Unsatisfied	45	18.75
Not applicable	8	3.33
Total	240	100

Source: Field Survey, 2011.

Students think that because of these services their results are improving. Coaching centers' teachers are friendlier and their teaching method is interesting. There are fewer students in coaching classes; so students can easily understand their lessons and solve their problems. Weekly model test and interaction among the students of different schools help them to survive in the competition. Some students also like suggestions and notes provided by the coaching centers. They think that better results can be possible by following these suggestions. List of these services are given into Table 5.16.

Table 5.16: Services of coaching centre preferred by the responde (Multiple responses are considered)

services	Frequency(n=232)	Percentage
Caring & friendly attitude of teachers	52	22.41
Proper understanding of lesson	69	29.74
Discipline & good environment	24	10.34
Weekly model test	61	26.29
Providing suggestions & notes	31	13.36
Proper caring for weak students	22	9.48
Teaching method	23	9.91
Interaction among the students of different school	10	4.31

Source: Field Survey, 2011.

However 150 students find satisfactory improvement in their results because of taking extra coaching. Another 53 students said that their results are moderately improved.

Table 5.17: Impact of coaching on students' result

Impact	Frequency	Percentage
Good	150	62.5
Moderate	53	22.08
Not improved	29	12.08
No applicable	8	3.33
Total	240	100

Source: Field Survey, 2011.

Present study finds a correlation between result and their involvement in the coaching. 174 students said they are satisfied with the service of coaching center and 150 students observed satisfactory improvement in their result.

This research has a hypothesis: **Students' results are positively related to their engagement in the coaching centre.** There is a strong positive relationship between students' result and their engagement in the coaching; r = 0.93; t = 2.53 accepted at 1degree of freedom and 0.1 level of confidence (Appendix 4). Proper caring for weak students, making lesson easy and understandable, weekly model test, careful teaching are the main reasons that help students to improve their result.

5.5 Conclusions

Parents' concern and their education level, different kinds of institutional problems, desire for better result etc. play an important role to increase the dependency on education coaching. A general conception in the society is that higher the family income, higher the involvement in coaching centers. But it is not true. As the demand for education is high in the society, every family tries to give their children better education. If the formal institutions fail to fulfill their demand, they depend on informal coaching centers.

CHAPTER SIX
IMPACT OF EDUCATION COACHING: AN OPINION SURVEY

6.1 Introduction

Every activity creates a mark on the space. Its impact may be positive or negative. Experts from different strata of the society view the impact from different angle. Another way of understanding how education coaching is expanding and its impact on society is to analyze the opinions of experts. As mentioned earlier, present study largely depend on primary source of information. Apart from the authorities of coaching centers, students and guardians, an attempt has been taken to get information from national level experts how they view the problem. This chapter is designed to sketch the views of national level experts on different issues related with education coaching.

6.2 National Level Experts and Their Opinions

National level experts are chosen from different segment of the society who are directly or indirectly involved with education sector and research. All the experts consider education coaching as a problem and think that it is harmful for the students. They said that in their student life they were not familiar with such types of commercial coaching. Private tuition and group coaching were found in small scale. At that time schools were more careful to fulfill extra need of the students. If they need more, they shared it with classmates. Sometimes they took the help from their teachers but most of the time it was free of cost. All of them suggest stopping education coaching but their suggestions were different. However, the experts are categorized as follows:

1. Professional groups
2. Educationist groups
3. Journalist groups
4. Policy maker groups

Professional groups include principals of different school and college who are directly related with formal educational institutions. They consider that education coaching is harmful for the development of our education system. It is an unethical practice for the teachers who are involved in coaching business. But guardians are equally responsible as they think that better results can be achieved through extra coaching.

Educationist experts include the intellectual groups. They think that changes in the society demand different activities. Education coaching is the result of such changes. Demand and competition in education sector has been increasing with the increasing number of population. When formal institutions fail to satisfy students' demand, they depend on informal coaching. Though it is harmful for our education system, it is fulfilling the extra need of large number of students.

Journalist groups highlight that education coaching is not students' need; rather students and guardians are bound to follow it. Students' results are improving through extra coaching. So, many guardians think that it is the only way to secure good marks. This group thinks that the major reasons of growth and proliferation of education coaching are rooted in the socio-political condition of the country.

Policy maker groups consider it as a social problem that must be prohibited by imposing law. They also said that corruption has been increased in education sector due to commercial coaching.

Table 6.1 shows a brief summary of the opinions of national level experts.

Table 6.1: Summery of the opinions of national level expert

Major issues	Professional groups	Educationist groups	Journalist groups	Policy maker groups
Reason for proliferation of coaching	Increasing competition among the students; To achieve commercial profit	commercial	commercial	Commercial
Necessity of coaching	Not necessary	Not necessary	Not necessary	Unnecessary
Impact on formal education	Serious	Deteriorating the quality of education	Becoming counter pole	Becoming parallel
Impact on students' result	Improving but credit must go to formal educational institution	Improving but students lose creativity	Improving	No impact
Problem in the formal educational institution push students to take extra coaching	Formal institutions have problems but it is not the only reason.	Formal institutions have problems but there are some other problems that are interlinked	Formal institutions have problems but it is not the only reason.	Formal institutions have problems but it is manageable.
Students' family income act as a factor to their involvement in the coaching	Higher income groups are very interested to send their wards to coaching.	Family income is not a factor; coaching creates a demand.	Higher income groups are very interested but other group also send their wards to coaching	Higher income groups are more keen to send their wards to coaching

Evaluation of coaching centers' education	Not so good	Not satisfactory; Only teach the short cut method of passing exam.	Only teach the short cut method of passing exam.	Not standard
Negative consequences of education coaching	Students are becoming careless to classroom education.	Education expenses are increasing; students are losing their leisure period	Education expenses and corruption have been increased	Increasing corruption
How to stop	By imposing law	Before imposing law, quality of education must be improved	By imposing law	By imposing law

Source: Compiled from interviews, 2011.

Their views are elaborated under specific question in the following section:

On the question of growth and proliferation of coaching center: From 1980s coaching centre has begun to flourish. It aims to train-up students. But their commercial proliferation create problem and increase the expenses of education. Most of the respondents agree that growth and proliferation of the coaching center is based on the business ethics. Providing quality education is not their concerning issue. Some of the respondents said that education coaching exist in our culture from the very beginning of the history of education; at present it has changed its shape with the changing demand of the society.

On the question of necessity of education coaching: All the respondents said that coaching is not necessary in our education system. But their views were different. Professional groups think that coaching has made the education a business product. It is a threat to our education system. Intellectual groups think that coaching loses the creativity. Journalist groups think that it is waste of time both for the students and their guardians. They also said that it has reduced the recreation time and creativity. Policy maker groups said that coaching has introduced corruption in education arena.

On the question of impact of coaching on formal education: All the experts indicate to the negative impact. Professional groups said that teaching is a noble profession and nobody should make it business. Both students and teachers are being careless because of coaching. Sometimes students are getting good marks in an unethical way. Educationist experts said that it has deteriorated the quality of education Journalist groups think that it has become counter pole to the formal education. Because most of the students are attending the coaching centers more carefully than formal classes in the school. But educationist experts and professional group deny this opinion. They said that it has no ability to become counter pole to formal education institution. Policy maker groups said that it is becoming parallel to formal institutions as large number of students is dependent on it.

On the question of relationship between formal educational institutions' problem and growth of coaching centers: Majority of experts said that formal educational institutions have some serious problems but it is not the only cause of growth of coaching centre. One common reason identified by the experts is teacher students' ratio. Teacher students' ratio is very high in government and private schools and colleges. There is one teacher for sixty five or seventy five students. It is impossible for him to fulfill all students' need. Another problem is that most of the schools do not introduce any kind of creative activities to understand their students that bookish knowledge is not all. Professional groups think that guardians do not want to understand the problem; they want goods marks and send their children to the coaching centers. Educationists agree that there are problems and that problems are linked with one another. But teachers, students and guardians should conscious to reduce the dependency on coaching. Journalists groups think that authorities of the coaching centers have strong political base to continue their business. Formal institutional problems create only an opportunity for their growth. Policy maker groups think that schools may have problems but authorities should manage it to maintain the quality of education.

On the question of coaching centers' quality of education: Most of the experts said that quality is not satisfactory. Non professional teachers cannot maintain the quality. Coaching centers run by the professional teachers are better. Some of the experts told that it only teaches the students how to pass the examination and short-cut method of completing the course curriculum.

On the question of the relationship between students' result and their involvement in the coaching: Experts has confessed that coaching has a positive impact on students' result. But professional groups said that we should not deny the credit of formal institutions because it makes the base of a student. Others experts said that students' result is improving because of taking extra coaching but it does not mean that quality of education has improved. They said that good results are not the indicators of good quality of education. But unfortunately, we have no others indicators to measure the quality of education.

On the question of the relationship between family income and students' involvement in the coaching: It is true that guardians have to spend large amount of money for education coaching. Professional groups think that those who have money send their children to the coaching. Policy maker group support this view. Journalists think that family expenditure on education has been increased. Different income groups spend much on education coaching according to their ability. Educationist groups think that coaching has created a demand for its service; that is why large number of students are involved in education coaching.

On the question of the negative consequences of education coaching: Experts have identified number negative consequences. These are: (1) most of the coaching centers expand their business in an informal way and desire to escape formal rules and regulations, (2) students are bound to follow the system as they think there result is improving because of coaching, (3) both teacher and students are becoming careless to classroom education, (4) students are losing their leisure period and they do not have any time for creative work, (5) parents have to spend lion share of their income, (6) it has introduced corruption in the education sector, (7) it has made education a commercial product.

On the question of how to stop education coaching: All the experts said that education coaching should be stopped by imposing law. But before that improvement in formal educational institutions is necessary. Without improving the formal system, it will be unwise to ban the coaching centers.

6.3 Conclusions

Education coaching is a problem for the development of our education system. But at the same time it has created a demand for quality education. Experts' views indicate that quality must be improved but not by the coaching centers' education. Necessary steps should be taken to improve the quality of education; it will help to reduce the dependency on coaching.

CHAPTER SEVEN
SUMMARY AND CONCLUSIONS

7.1 Summary and Conclusions

Informal activity is a phenomenon mostly seen in the developing countries where population size is much higher. But at present it is growing in every corner of the globe though the pattern and shape vary from country to country. Education coaching as an informal activity has been flourishing since last two decades. This proliferation is very larger than any other parts of the country. Present research focuses on education coaching and its nature, development, students' involvement as well as their dependency on coaching. In this chapter an attempt has been taken to sketch the whole process in a single frame.

A recent phenomenon in Bangladesh informal sector is the expansion of coaching centers to provide organized private coaching to the students. It has now turned out to be a lucrative business. A huge number of students are getting services through informal education coaching. So, it is necessary to understand this sector whether the sector stands as counter pole of the formal education sector. Present research is an attempt to explore the dynamic of this sector. It aims to investigate the process of growth of coaching centers as informal activity and its role in the city economy. It also tries to know the size of economy of this sector, process of getting students' involvement and the proportion of the students come through these coaching centers. Present research is mainly based on primary source of information as the study is unique in nature. Primary data was collected by an empirical data survey through checklists. Checklists were used for authorities of the coaching centers, students and their parents. This study also considered experts' opinions through interview.

Historical evidence shows that education coaching was prevailed in our culture from the very beginning. But it had different form and different motive from the present day commercial coaching centers. Educations coaching through commercial coaching centers have started their activities since 1980s. Different types of coaching centers have been identified throughout the research; their nature and characteristics differ from one another. Scanning their advertisements and promotional activities, their attachment with their association, legal status, the study considers that one hundred and twenty three coaching centers are operating their business in Dhaka city. If their branches are considered, the number will be five to six times greater. Most of these are located in Farmgate area. But their mushrooming growth have been found all around the city. For the detailed study, twenty coaching centers have been selected. These were categorized as academic and admission coaching. Significant characteristics have been identified: most of the coaching centers have more than one branch. But the coordination system among the branches is not so good. Outside of Dhaka the branches work more or less independently than the branches in Dhaka. Total number of employee is not fixed and they do not have fixed hour of operation. Wage structure varies from one coaching center to another and it is not fixed. Very few coaching centers have professional teachers (who are previously or currently involved in schools or colleges). All the coaching centers have those teachers who are still students of universities and colleges. A large portion of students are getting their services from these coaching centers and the number is increasing dramatically day by day.

It is found that huge amount of money is rolling in this sector. But they have to invest little amount of money to start their business. Income source of coaching centers is different types of fees that they collect from the students. Their average net turnover is 14 percent and the highest range is more than 21 percent. One the major reasons behind the proliferation of these coaching centers is that it is a profitable business where investment is nominal but the return is phenomenal.

Coaching centers provide different types of services. They are successful to create demand for their services. But present research has identified some other factors that push the students to take extra education coaching. One such factor is the problems in formal educational institutions. Formal institutions have different types of problems. One major problem is that teacher students' ratio. Most of the institutions do not maintain an ideal ratio. The ratio is 1:65 or 1:75. Other infrastructural problems disappoint the students. They feel the need of extra coaching. Present study found that all these problems are directly associated with the growth of coaching center (x^2 =1.31 accepted at 1degree of freedom and .05 level of confidence). That means problems in the formal institutions create a base for the growth of coaching centers. A misconception about the coaching is that higher the family income higher the involvement of students in the coaching. But it is not true. The study hypothesis (Students' family income is directly related to their involvement in the coaching) was rejected. Study found that family income do not play a major role. Whatever the family income, the large portions of it spend for extra education coaching. Both parents and students' results are improving because of extra coaching. Present study found a strong relationship between students' results and their engagement in the coaching (r = 0.93; t = 2.53 accepted at 1degree of freedom and 0.1 level of confidence).

This research also tries to find out the impact of education coaching. National level experts gave opinion on this issue. Similarities and dissimilarities have been found among the views of national experts. All the experts identified the growth of coaching centers as a problem. They said that it has a negative impact on the formal education as well as students' creativity. They are not satisfied with quality of coaching centers' education. They have pointed out that it is necessary to stop the education coaching by imposing law. But before that the quality of formal education must be improved.

To sum up, it can be said that education coaching as one of the largest informal sector activities expands its sphere of activity all around the city. Large numbers of students are getting their informal services through these coaching centers. But large scale proliferation of this activity creates negative consequences on our formal education.

7.2 Guideline for Futher Research

For the limited scope of the M.S. research, all parts of this sector are not explained in the present study. More elaborate study is necessary to explain the dynamics of this sector. Present study considers the organized coaching centers only. A separate study is necessary to examine other education coaching (Private tuition and group coaching) to know the actual workforce involve in this sector. Present study finds out the reasons behind students' dependency on education coaching. So the next step of research is to identify the flow of students (from where they come and which coaching centers they choose).

REFERENCES

Aggarwal, J.C. (2000), "Education Reforms in India for The 21st Century", New Delhi: Shipra publications.

Ahmed, S (1986), "Dacca: A study in Urban History and Development", London: Curzon Press.

Bangladesh Bureau of Statistics (BBS) (2001) Bangladesh Population Census, 2001, National series, Vol.1, Urban Area Report, Dhaka: Ministry of Planning. Government of Bangladesh.

Banlapedia (2006), The National Encyclopedia of Bangladesh, Vol.5, p.444-458. Dhaka: Asiatic Society of Bangladesh.

Banlapedia (2006), The National Encyclopedia of Bangladesh, Vol.9, p.135-140. Dhaka: Asiatic Society of Bangladesh.

International Labour Office (2002), "Women and Men in the Informal Economy: A Statistical Picture", Geneva: Employment Sector, International Labour Office, New York: Oxford University Press.

Kalliski, J. (1999) "Everyday Urbanism", New York: Monacelli Press.

Kotler, P. (2006), "Marketing Management", USA: Printice Hall.

Sathuraman, S.V. (1977), "The Informal Sector in Developing Countries Employment, Poverty and Environment", International Lobour Office: Geneva.

Raymont, T (1963), "Modern Education: Its Aims and Methods", New York: MacGraw- Hill & Co.

"The Daily Star", page 14, 22nd August, 2010.

Oxford Advanced Learner's Dictionary (8th edition) 2010, Oxford University Press

Appendix 1

LIST OF COACHING CENTERS			
SL NO.	NAME	LOCATION	CATEGORY
1	UCC	FARMGATE	ADMISSION
2	U@C	FARMGATE	ADMISSION
3	POGITRON	FARMGATE	ADMISSION
4	CLASSIC	FARMGATE	ADMISSION
5	ELIS	FARMGATE	ADMISSION
6	VARSITY COACHING	FARMGATE	ADMISSION
7	OMECA	FARMGATE	ADMISSION
8	FOCUS	FARMGATE	ADMISSION
9	SUNRISE	FARMGATE	ADMISSION
10	PROCOUSHOLI	FARMGATE	ADMISSION
11	UDVAS	FARMGATE	ADMISSION, ACADEMY
12	3DOCTORS' ACADEMY	FARMGATE	ADMISSION
13	SUVECHCHA	FARMGATE	ADMISSION
14	PRIMATE	FARMGATE	ADMISSION
15	RETINA	FARMGATE	ADMISSION
16	MAF'S MEDICITY	FARMGATE	ADMISSION
17	ADMISSION PLUS	FARMGATE	ADMISSION
18	UNIAID	FARMGATE	ADMISSION
19	SAIC COACHING	INDIRA ROAD,FARMGATE	ACADEMIC
20	STANDARD COACHING	W. TEJTURIPARA, FARMGATE	ACADEMIC
21	CONCRETE COACHING	E. TEJTURIPARA, FARMGATE	ADMISSION
22	CONFIRM	E. TEJTURIPARA, FARMGATE	ADMISSION
23	SUCCESS COACHING	INDIRA ROAD,FARMGATE	ADMISSION
24	EFUM COACHING	INDIRA ROAD,FARMGATE	ACADEMIC
25	GENUINE TUTORIAL	INDIRA ROAD,FARMGATE	ACADEMIC
26	MABS COACHING	GREEN ROAD	ACADEMIC
27	RENAISSANCE	DHANMONDI	ACADEMIC
28	PROFFESOR'S ACADEMY	DHANMONDI	ACADEMIC
29	3 STAR ACADEMY	DHANMONDI	ACADEMIC
30	BUETEC	SCIENCE LABORATORY	ACADEMIC
31	OXYGEN	SCIENCE LABORATORY	ACADEMIC
32	ENGLISH FOR ACDEMIC CARE	SCIENCE LABORATORY	ACADEMIC

Appendix 2

Table 1 Distribution of subjects taking for extra coaching(multiple responses)

Subjects	Frequency(n=232)	Percentage
English	164	70.69
Bangla	58	25
General math.	201	86.64
Higher math.	90	38.79
Physics	63	27.16
Chemistry	60	25.86
Biology	34	14.66
Social science	39	16.81
General science	80	34.48
Islamic studies	28	12.07
Accounting	17	7.33
Agriculture	11	4.74
Drawing	3	1.29
Sanskrit	1	0.43

Source: Field Survey,2011

Appendix 3

Box 5.2: Hypothesis test (Regression analysis)

Let us define the linear regression model as,

$$X_i = \alpha_i + \beta_i y_i + \mu_i$$

where,

X_i = No. of family

α_i = the intercept term

β_i = Regression coefficient or Beta coefficient

y_i = No. of students involved in coaching

μ_i = the residual term

Regression analysis

ANOVA[b]

Model		Sum of Squares	df	Mean Square	F	Sig.
1	Regression	1177.934	1	1177.934	12.538	.009[a]
	Residual	657.621	7	93.946		
	Total	1835.556	8			

a. Predictors: (Constant), No. of family (X)

b. Dependent Variable: No. of students involved in coaching (y)

At 1 and 8 degree of freedom and .05 level of confidence the critical value of F is 5.318. It is greater than the calculated value (F= 12.538). So, we may reject *Ho:* students' family income is directly related to their involvement in the extra education coaching, at 5% level of significance. Students' family income is not directly related to their involvement in the extra education coaching.

Appendix 4

H₃ : Students' results are positively related to their engagement in the coaching centre.

Box 5.3: Hypothesis test (t test)

Calculation for coefficient of correlation

Opinion	Students' involvement in the coaching and their satisfaction (X)	X^2	Impact on students' result (Y)	Y^2	XY
Satisfactory	174	30276	150	22500	26100
Moderate	13	169	53	2809	689
Unsatisfactory	45	2025	29	841	1305
Total	232	32470	232	26150	28094

$$r = \frac{N\sum XY - \sum X\sum Y}{\sqrt{\{N\sum X^2 - (\sum X)^2\}\{N\sum Y^2 - (\sum Y)^2\}}}$$

$$= \frac{(3\times28094)-(232\times232)}{\sqrt{\{(3\times32470)-(232)^2\}\{(3\times26150)-(232)^2\}}}$$

$$= \frac{30458}{\sqrt{43586\times24626}} = 0.93$$

r= 0.93 indicates a strong positive relationship.

t test : $t = \frac{r\sqrt{N-2}}{\sqrt{1-r^2}} = \frac{0.93\sqrt{3-2}}{\sqrt{1-(0.93)^2}} = 2.53$

At 1 degree of freedom and 0.1 level of confidence the critical value of t is 3.078. It is greater than the calculated value. So, the hypothesis is accepted.

Appendix 5

SL	Name	Affiliation
1	Professor Harun-er Rashid	Pro Vice Chancellor, Dhaka University
2	Professor Nazrul Islam	Former Chairman, UGC
3	Dr. Abdul Malek	Professor, I.E.R., Dhaka University
4	Fahima Khatun	Chairman, Education Board of Dhaka
5	Rashed Khan Menon	Chairman, Parliamentary Standing Committee on MoE
6	Mr. Khalilur Rahman	Additional Secretary, MoPME
7	Mr. Rakib –ur -Rahman	Joint Secretary, MoE
8	Mr. Sarower Mahmud	Deputy Secretary, MoPME
9	Manju Ara Begum	Privipal, Viqurunnesa Noon School and College
10	Father Benjamin de Costa	Principal, Notredem, College
11	Md. Abu Syed Bhuiya	Principal, Govt. Laboratory High School
12	Md. Shahidul Islam Biswas	Principal, Agrani School and College
13	Md,. Mujibar Rahman	Principal, New Poltan Line School and College
14	Md. Anisul Haque	Deputy Editor, The Daily Prothom Alo
15	Md. Mokammel Hossain	Assistant Editor, The Daily Jugantor
16	Md. Shafiqur Rahman	Journalist, The Daily Sun